AF255805

The Best Fruit

The Best Fruit

*How Raising Your Emotional Intelligence
Helps Spiritual Development*

JACQUELYN M. RAGIN

WIPF & STOCK · Eugene, Oregon

THE BEST FRUIT
How Raising Your Emotional Intelligence Helps Spiritual Development

Wipf & Stock
An Imprint of Wipf and Stock Publishers
199 W. 8th Ave., Suite 3
Eugene, OR 97401

www.wipfandstock.com

PAPERBACK ISBN: 978-1-6667-8400-8
HARDCOVER ISBN: 978-1-6667-8401-5
EBOOK ISBN: 978-1-6667-8402-2

VERSION NUMBER 11/01/23

"But the fruit of the Spirit is love, joy, peace, patience, kindness, goodness, faithfulness, gentleness, self-control; against such things there is no law" (Gal 5:22–23).

Contents

Introduction

"But the fruit of the Spirit is love, joy, peace, patience, kindness, goodness, faithfulness, gentleness, self-control; against such things there is no law" (Gal 5:22–23).

ABOUT THE TITLE: I asked myself, if I had a fruit tree, what would I want for my labor? Answer: "The best fruit and the highest yield, superior fruit and the biggest net gain." We live in the land of opportunity, yet so many people fall short of life goals due to their inability to manage their emotions. I am continually amazed at how low emotional intelligence sabotages success these days. Young professionals or would-be professionals lose contracts, money, relationships, personal freedom, and peace of mind due to their inability to manage their emotions and successfully handle the emotions of other people. Successful living even eludes many of my senior counterparts for the same reason. They're experiencing low or no return on their investment of time, energy, and even money due to low emotional management.

"In public life, people seem to be growing more strident and confrontational, and less respectful and trusting. Cable news and political rallies are the clearest exemplars of this trend. In churches, as well, people's capacity to work through conflicts in a way that does not leave them feeling wounded and defensive has deteriorated."[1]

---

1. Kelsey, *Practicing Civility*, 146.

I also marvel at how poorly managers are trained to lead. Leaders in today's world need great human resource skills along with the ability to manage their own emotions. Patience, self-control, and resilience are valued highly in the job market, yet love, peace, gentleness, and kindness are not so much. These are godly attributes that add to being a successful people manager.

Throughout my years in ministry, I have committed to increasing my emotional intelligence to improve my ability to handle life's challenges and grow in my relationships, both professional and personal. After taking a continuing education class in emotional intelligence, I became interested in the subject and went on to earn a certificate. I wrote this book because of what I see every day in the world we live in. Young people in particular struggle to keep jobs, maintain good relationships, stay in school, and be progressive professionally due largely in part to low emotional intelligence. During my many years as a pastor I met individuals of all ages who have attempted to lead others while failing to handle their own emotions in ways that cause those whom they lead to want to engage with them.

Developing high EI can lead to greater spiritual development, thus adding potential for success in a person's life, leadership ability, and personal relationships. I recommend that Christians leaders develop their emotional intelligence with the intent of augmenting the work of the Holy Spirit. The Holy Spirit is God within the life of the believer, at work to bring the individual into the image of Jesus Christ. The Holy Spirit is often referred to as the change agent who cultivates the "fruit of the Spirit." We all need help when attempting to grow and change. We should expect our higher power to be active and enabling in our attempt to become our best selves, being able to successfully lead and navigate life's challenges and opportunities.

High emotional intelligence is key to successful relationship building, personal development, and adopting a healthy mindset. "People with well-developed emotional skills are more likely to be content and effective in their lives, mastering the habits of mind that foster their own productivity, people who cannot marshal some control over their emotional life fight inner battles that sabotage their ability for focused work and clear thought."[2]

Peter Salovey and John Mayer describe emotional intelligence as the ability to "recognize, understand, and manage our own emotions. Recognize, understand, and influence the emotions of others." Daniel Goleman in the 1990s defined it as "The capacity for recognizing our own feelings and those of others, for motivating ourselves, and for managing emotions well in ourselves and in our relationships."[3]

As a student of the science of emotional intelligence I've discovered that the characteristics of high emotional intelligence mesh well with the fruit of the Spirt the apostle Paul advocates for every Christian to adopt in order to live the Christian life. The Holy Spirit is the change agent who will produce fruit that will lead to abundant living and great leadership potential. Practicing what will increase your emotional intelligence adds to the cultivation process.

I agree with social scientists who believe EI can be learned and developed. Also, I believe the fruit of the Spirit is cultivated for and to the benefit of the believer and the world. Both are developmental processes, one developed spiritually and one developed emotionally. Psychology cannot be ignored in spiritual maturation, and support can be found in Paul's own words: "think on these things." "Study," Paul says, meaning concentrate and feed your mind as well as your spirit. He also wrote "love the Lord with all your heart, soul, and mind".

Cultivation is defined as attempting to acquire or develop something. A farmer cultivates the ground to produce a crop. He or she tills, fertilizes, waters, and installs support. Fruit, as Paul is using the term, is a metaphor for the result that God produces in a person who submits to him. Christians are required to submit to the Spirit of God so that "fruit will be produced" in them. It will be evident to those who see and have relationship with you that God is at work in your life. That does not mean that we as Christians don't have work to do. Every revelation requires a response lest we

2. Goleman, *Emotional Intelligence*, 36.

3. Goleman, *Emotional Intelligence*, 36.

stall the work of the Spirit. It is up to us to do what will increase our emotional intelligence and thereby enhance the work of the Spirit. Practicing increasing your emotional intelligence will augment the work of the Holy Spirit.

Social scientists agree that the ability to manage one's emotions and the emotions of other people is crucial to being a great, successful, consistent, mentally stable leader. While it is possible to increase your emotional intelligence without developing spiritually, it is better in the long run to also be spiritually grounded if not for your own well-being, then for the sake of your relationships with God and other people. When you meet overwhelming challenges in life, you will need something greater than yourself to help you not just through but to internalize what happens in those circumstances in a way that makes you a better person.

I grew up sandwiched in age between two genius brothers. What set me apart from my oldest sibling was my desire to not let my shortcomings prohibit me from accomplishing my goals. Self-management was a priority. Little did I know that practicing how to manage my emotions would set me up to well manage challenges in adult life. My dad practiced the same and shared good advice with me that I took to heart. He stressed temperance and was extremely self-motivated, owning, and successfully managing, a delivery service he started himself.

As a pastor I observed firsthand the struggles of parishioners who lacked self-control, emotional well-being, and professional growth. My position afforded me a front-row seat to the personal accomplishments and growth of church members who were living their lives successfully. Since I knew them well, I could see that IQ alone was not the determining factor in their successful living and professional achievements. When I read my first book on emotional intelligence I was not surprised to learn that emotional intelligence contributed largely to personal success. What surprised me, though, is how well the fundamentals of EI paired with the fruit of the Spirit. Self-awareness, temperance, self-motivation, and empathy are the attributes of high emotional intelligence compared to the fruit of the Spirit, which is love, joy, self-control, peace, patience (long suffering), goodness (gentleness), and faithfulness.

Social scientists have studied predictors of success: personality, education, IQ, and opportunity. Yet those of us who have served in a pastoral capacity have discovered that these determinates alone don't account for the successes of some of the people whom we have pastored. Faith does play a large role in successes, but faith alone does not lead to achievement. One can be a good person yet have no self-motivation or be a faithful person yet lack high self-awareness. I hope this book will enlighten and inspire leaders interested in being their best emotionally intelligent and spiritually grounded selves while leading others.

"Emotional intelligence matters in pastoral leadership because ministry is all about relationships and because emotional intelligence is not static, it is of vital importance to anyone who seeks to train and equip pastoral leaders. We have seen failures of pastoral leadership in recent years across various theological traditions around the world. Rarely have these been the result of a poorly delivered sermon or an incorrectly parsed verb."[4]

What stressed me when working with young ministry leaders was their propensity to bite the hands that fed them. Their lack of temperance often resulted in lost opportunities, petty crime, bad relationships and a general "falling out" with God. I hope this book helps someone consider how increasing their EI can not only contribute to the good fruit that God cultivates but considers its potential to assist them in successfully navigating life and relationships.

---

4. Kimmons and White, *Clergy Education*, 371.

1

What is Emotional Intelligence?

"The daily challenge of dealing effectively with emotions is critical to the human condition because our brains are hard-wired to give emotions the upper hand." Travis Bradberry

TRAVIS BRADBERRY IS TALENT Smart's founder. In his book *Emotional Intelligence 2.0*, co-written with Jean Greaves, he writes, "The daily challenge of dealing effectively with emotions is critical to the human condition because our brains are hard-wired to give emotions the upper hand." He goes on to explain that our senses send signals to the brain: "They enter your brain at the base near the spinal cord but must travel to your frontal lobe (behind your forehead) before reaching the place where rational, logical thinking takes place. The trouble is they pass through your limbic system along the way—the place where emotions are produced."[1] This journey ensures you experience things emotionally before your reason can kick in gear. The communication between your emotional and rational brains is the physical source of emotional intelligence."

1. Bradberry and Graves, *Emotional Intelligence 2.0*, 6.

Richard Boyatzis and Annie McGee explain, "The neural systems responsible for the intellect and for the emotions are separate, but they have intimately interwoven connections. The brain circuitry that interweaves thought and feelings provides the neutral basis of primal leadership. And, despite the great value that business culture often places on an intellect devoid of emotion, our emotions are, in a very real sense, more powerful than our intellect. In moments of emergency, our emotional centers—the limbic brain—commandeer the rest of the brain."[2]

Roy Oswald further explains in his work *Emotional Intelligent and Congregational Leadership*, "When emotional intelligence is operating at a high level, dozens of interchanges happen every minute between the neocortex and the limbic brain. This interchange results in people making the most appropriate response to most emotionally laden circumstances."[3]

Daniel Goleman in the 1990s listed the fundamentals of high emotional intelligence and separated them into five domains:

- Self-awareness: "Recognizing a feeling as it happens—a keystone of emotional intelligence."[4] High self-awareness involves objectivity, self-evaluation and recognizing triggers.

- Temperance (also called self-management): Managing one's own emotions can prevent at the very least the likelihood of being a victim of one's own ill-advised decisions based on impulse.

- Self-motivation: "Marshalling emotions in the service of a goal is essential for paying attention, for self-motivation and mastery and for creativity."[5]

- Empathy: Goleman describes "another ability that builds on emotional self-awareness, the fundamental "people skill."[6]

---

2. Boyatzis and McKee, *Resonant Leadership*, 25.

3. Oswald, *Emotional Intelligence*, 105.

4. Goleman, *Emotional Intelligence*, 37.

5. Goleman, *Emotional Intelligence*, 37.

6. Goleman, *Emotional Intelligence*, 37.

- Social skills (or handling relationships): Goleman defines social skills, saying, "The art of relationships is, in large part skill in managing others. . . People who excel in these skills do well at anything that relies on interacting smoothly with others; they are social stars."[7]

Empathy is a crucial characteristic to ministry. It is a requirement to be a good Christian and leader. "But when it comes to business, we rarely hear people raised, let alone rewarded, for their empathy. The very word seems un-businesslike, out of place amid the tough realities of the marketplace."[8] I was once told I would never make it in the corporate world because I was too empathetic and concerned about fairness.

Salvoey and Mayer list five domains divided into three groups:

- Personal competence

- Self-awareness

- Self-management

- Self-motivation.

- Social competence

- Social awareness. Recognizing how others feel. Being able to "read the room."

- Relationship management

Self-awareness is knowing or recognizing how we feel: being aware of being triggered or emotionally influenced. Self-awareness needs to be developed during childhood. "From self-awareness—understanding one's emotions and being clear about one's purpose—flows self-management, the focused drive that all leaders need to achieve their goals. Without knowing what we're feeling we're at a loss to manage those feelings; instead, our emotions control us."[9]

7. Goleman, *Emotional Intelligence*, 37.

8. Goleman et al., *Primal Leadership*, 49.

9. Goleman., et al., *Primal Leadership*, 45.

Self-motivation is the ability to move oneself to action. Self-motivation comes from one's desire to act and is key to working autonomously, moving past obstacles and leading in difficult situations.

On relationship management: "The triad of self-awareness, self-management, and empathy all come together in the final EI ability: relationship management. Here we find the most visible tools of leadership-persuasion, conflict management, and collaboration among them. Managing relationships skillfully boils down to handling other people's emotions. This, in turn, demands that leaders be aware of their own emotions and attuned with empathy to the people they lead."[10]

The world of Christian ministry is no different than the business arena when it comes to emotional intelligence. I have personally watched ministers and pastors wreck their relationships due to their unwillingness to address what is really at the root of their angst. Symptoms are not root causes. Inability to handle being offended also has derailed some ministry leaders. Offense can lead to anger, resentment, jealousy, and other negative emotions. Many churches have been started by ministers who were offended and chose to start their own church rather than put offense in its place.

Now, more than ever, people are creating their own ministries. Like business owners, the creator can be their own worst employee. Leading your ministry, like leading a business, requires discipline, self-awareness, and sacrifice. I have met ministry leaders who have not put the work into raising their self-awareness and/or relationship skills yet they hope to thrive, believing God will change them. God changes what we lend ourselves to.

There are ministers who break away from organizations to start their own ministries yet have not mastered any human resource skills. A friend of mine left a church along with several other church members because of what they perceived as bad leadership. They formed their own church. Pride and arrogance led them to believe they could provide good leadership and pastoral care despite none of them being experienced preachers, having

10. Goleman et al., *Primal Leadership*, 51.

an appropriate regard for women in leadership or any spiritual formation credentials. Being a pastor is much harder than it appears. After several months it became apparent to them no one in the group had the leadership and preaching skills needed for good church communion and continuity. Rather than hire someone to be pastor they all eventually left to join other ministries, blaming each other for the new church's demise.

Yet others who have good experiences while under the leadership of their mentor flounder once on their own. An associate of mine started a church, and though she had financial support and spiritual guidance from her church denomination, she had trouble relating to people. She was excellent being of assistance to her mentor but lacked the skills necessary for good pastoral leadership. Though some of her associates attempted to provide the best advice on how to grow her ministry, she didn't listen and instead became defensive. She alienated friends that advised her to adjust in how she addressed pastoral concerns. Eventually my associate became emotionally overwhelmed, and despite her best attempts, the church folded.

It is not surprising to find that people who intentionally work for and by themselves often struggle to maintain lasting business relationships. Working alone may be the mode of operation that works best for them, though if their challenges are due to low emotional intelligence, the struggle can interfere with long-term success. To what degree their challenges are overcome relies largely on their willingness and ability to grow and endure.

I hired a contractor to work on my house. It was during the pandemic, and contractors were not only overwhelmed with work, but construction materials were hard to obtain. It took a while to locate a contractor that was available. The project manager called shortly after I messaged him and I was a little surprised when he said the contractor could start work right away.

My experience was great initially, but it unfortunately turned into a nightmare. The contractor wouldn't follow up on my concerns about how some of the work was being done. The project manager mentioned that he had hoped the contractor would improve on how he responded to customer issues, then, in the middle of my project, quit working for the guy. The most disturbing thing about the contractor's behavior was how he would become upset with my requests for him to send someone back to my house to complete or correct work. He would yell eventually, saying that I was harassing him and blaming me for bothering him about things he promised to address.

After experiencing one of his tirades, I demanded he not yell at me and do business in a professional manner. Though I demanded he never speak to me in a demeaning tone, I realized he was beyond able to control his emotions. It has been eighteen months since the project started, and the contractor has yet to complete the work.

THERE IS A DISTINCT DIFFERENCE BETWEEN EI AND IQ

IQ test vs. EQ tests

- IQ tests measure your cognitive (academic) ability.

- EI tests measure emotional management.

- EI prepares you for life.

- IQ offers no preparation for life's challenges.

- IQ can be genetic and possibly environmental.

- EI can be improved and developed.

My brothers had higher IQs than myself, yet I was able to launch out on my own at a young age, secure my first apartment, and even help my younger brother secure his own living space when he needed it. I bought my first car, while still in high school, with my own money and graduated at age 17. Perseverance, self-awareness, and hard work largely contributed to my ability to obtain what I wanted.

2

Fruit of the Spirit

"But the fruit of the Spirit is love, joy, peace, patience, kindness, goodness, faithfulness, gentleness, self-control; against such things there is no law" (Gal 5:22–23).

IN THIS PASSAGE OF scripture from the Christian Bible, the writer, apostle Paul, is informing the hearers of his letter that the result of seeking what is not Christ-like is sinful and has unwanted consequences, but Christian virtues promote freedom. Paul was one of the most influential spiritual leaders of his time, and his letters in the Christian Bible teach and inspire to this day.

Living a life being guided by the Spirit of God Paul calls "walking in the Spirit." The evidence of "walking in and by the Spirit" Paul calls "the fruit of the Spirit". That evidence is described as love, joy, peace, patience, kindness, goodness, faithfulness, gentleness, self-control. Paul is speaking from his own experiences and encounters with God and uses images of fruit in his explanation due to the agricultural economy the hearers were accustomed to. Paul wrote the fruit of the Spirit is evidence that God is at work in the believer.

"As fruit is the product of the tree so also is spiritual fruit the product of the spirit-filled life. So what Paul is saying with his beautiful qualities is this: these are the qualities that God himself will produce in a person's every day, ordinary human life because the life of God himself is at work within them."[1]

"The Fruit of the Spirit in Galatians (5:22) refers specifically to the Holy Spirit, and the spiritual gifts that are given to every believer, and the quality the Holy Spirit develops in the life of the believer."[2] "The Holy Spirit has been given to Christians to lead and empower them and indicate an undeniable relationship with Christ. The fruit of the Spirit is the result of having the Holy Spirit in one's life. To bear the fruit of the Spirit is the vocation of the world as a testimony to God's continued presence and work on the world"[3]

Love

Love is the first virtue Paul lists. Love is the essence of God himself. It is no wonder why Paul would say that God himself would produce in the Christian his own essence and reason for creating mankind. Love is the attribute of God that brings us in relationship with him, and love should be the main reason we serve mankind. Christians are called to a life of service to humankind and the rational for doing so should be love. Paul writes in 1 Cor 13:3–7, "And if I give away all my possessions *to charity*, and if I surrender my body so that I may glory, but do not have love, it does me no good." Paul explains that all the other spiritual gifts and gestures are good, but if love is not motivation, then the effort is wasted, even sinful.

Paul requests us to "Love the Lord with your heart, mind and soul" (Deut 6:5), which is one of the multiple commandments given to Moses for God's people to follow. The heart is where love resides. The mind is the emotional epicenter of your being. Why

1. Wright, *Cultivating the Fruit*, 22.

2. McQuerry and Kostenberger, as cited in Montaudon-Tomas, 22.

3. Kenneson, *Life on the Vine*, 19.

wouldn't Paul include the mind if he believes Christians should love with their whole being?

Paul further describes love in this passage: "Love is patient, love is kind, it is not jealous; love does not brag, it is not arrogant. It does not act disgracefully, it does not seek its own *benefit*; it is not provoked, does not keep an account of a wrong *suffered*, it does not rejoice in unrighteousness, but rejoices with the truth; it keeps every confidence, it believes all things, hopes all things, endures all things" (1 Cor 13:4).

Joy

Some scholars of EI may not consider joy a core value, yet it is an essential element to living a life of happiness. Many rich people have amassed fortunes, yet joy eludes them. Joy in this context that Paul discusses is for the good of all the community, yet if joy is not internal, lasting happiness can be difficult to achieve. Joy can be achieved by serving and sharing with others. Sharing is one way to cause joy, and empathy is required for sharing from the heart.

Peace

"Peace is wholeness in one's soul where all the parts fit together; there is no inner conflict giving the peaceful person not only the ability to have confidence during pressure but also the presence of mind to make effective decisions to bring change amid trouble. Joy and peace are intimately connected, with joy bringing inner confidence during pressure while peace brings the ability to move forward to address the pressure in a positive way."[4]

Peace is at its highest value when it is absent from either the environment or the mind. Peace can be the absence of emotional conflict or the result of reestablishing a connection. Peace can also be described as the absence of war or bringing resolution or the answer to a problem. Peace within adds to the good of a community.

4. Crowther, *Fruit of the Spirit*, 27.

The peace that Paul is referring to comes by faith. At age thirty-two I decided to get married. My reasons were rational, but my choice of partner was not. After considerable contemplation I felt peace about it. That peace came from the decision being settled in my mind and the courage I had mustered to go through with it. The decision didn't produce a good result, and I learned that the peace spawned from concluding is not the same as the peace of God. Peace of which Paul refers comes with the promises of God. Peace also comes from surrender and the realization that things you can't change by yourself your higher power can handle. Peace can be derived from spiritual discipline and walking in the Spirit.

In the book of Numbers, God told the prophet Moses to tell Aaron, the priest, to pronounce a blessing and peace over the people: "The LORD bless you and keep you; The LORD cause His face to shine on you, And be gracious to you; The LORD lift up His face to you, And give you peace" (Num 6:26). Peace was a valuable commodity then and still is. Along with the blessing of *shalom* should be "keep the faith." Faith and hope contribute to peace. Trust and hope can carry you through the challenges of life.

Self-Control

Self-control is the ability to manage impulses and emotions and exhibit behavior that is non-threatening. Self-control doesn't seem like a popular topic these days. The ability to manage and maintain one's composure doesn't seem as important as in times past. Though people with high self-control are viewed as more responsible and trustworthy than those who don't have it, just the opposite seems to be what is most popular on social media. Social media provides an audience for bad behavior attributed to low impulse control. The need for attention by some due to loneliness, or overall rejection by society, is exacerbated rather than met. Reactions to posts are often negative and can lead to ongoing virtual disputes that can end tragically.

Road rage happens frequently these days, and gunfire has increased significantly over the last ten years. Gun battles to settle disputes and gain revenge have become commonplace in American society. Generation Z employees walk off the job or quietly quit rather than stay and manage their relationships with employers. To make things worse, we live in an age of bad role models. Behavior that society once deemed unacceptable is now common and acceptable. The Bible speaks about such behavior. Below are some Scriptures that explain the results of low self-control:

Proverbs 25:28—"Like a city that is broken into *and* without walls, *so* is a person who has no self-control over his spirit."

First Corinthians 9:25—"Everyone who competes in the games exercises self-control in all things. So, they do it to obtain a perishable wreath, but we can imperishable (something spiritually greater)."

As Christians we are to put into practice outstanding social skills. Colossians 3:12 reads "So, as those who have been chosen of God, holy and beloved, put on a heart of compassion, kindness, humility, gentleness, and patience."

Gentleness

Gentleness can be described as good nature in action. It may be motivated by kindness and or love. It is the application of the other gifts and can include mercy. The motivation for gentleness may also be to avoid breakage or to promote trust or confidence. While working as a technician I had an unexpected personal encounter with a shop supervisor. I learned, while on the phone at work, my brother had committed suicide. I had a complete meltdown a few yards from the shop floor where other employees were working, including a supervisor I wasn't fond of. Upon hearing me in distress he ran to me and helped me up from the floor into a nearby office. He spoke to me with gentleness and assurance, which caught me off guard. The shocking news about my brother had me reeling, yet during that event the supervisor's actions stood out. He attempted to minister to me, though we weren't close, and later that morning drove me to my mother's house, even encouraging me as he left to return to work.

Faithfulness

"Faithfulness is the attribute of one who is loyal, who keeps commitments that have been made even when it is difficult. This leader is a person who not only fulfills the proper responsibilities but is a person of integrity. The most basic definition of integrity is honesty and consistency between a person's values and behavior and that the person is trustworthy."[5]

Christians are commanded to remain committed to God and Christian values, not wavering. We're required to keep showing up for ourselves and others. Constant loyalty and devotion is God's way of showing his love, and he expects the same in return. The Christian Bible is full of God's promises, and by keeping them he models the behavior Paul refers to in the passage concerning the fruit of the Spirit. Psalms 37:3 comes with a promise: "Trust in the Lord and do good; Live in the land and cultivate faithfulness. Delight yourself in the Lord; And He will give you the desires of your heart. Commit your way to the Lord, Trust also in Him, and He will do it. He will bring out your righteousness as the light, And your judgment as the noonday" (Ps 37:3).

Patience

Patience is the ability to wait. Wright defines patience as, "The ability to endure for a long time whatever opposition and suffering may come our way, and to show perseverance without wanting retaliation or revenge. The ability to put up with the weaknesses and foibles of others (including other beliefs) and to show forbearance toward them, without getting quickly irritated or angry enough to want to fight back."[6]

Perseverance in some translations of the Bible is substituted for the word "patience." Patience and perseverance can be used interchangeably when describing the process of waiting and enduring. Yet perseverance requires action other than just waiting when

---

5. Yukl, as cited by Crowther, *Fruit of the Spirit*, 33.

6. Wright, *Cultivating the Fruit*, 69.

trying to obtain something. One can be a good, patient Christian yet lack perseverance. A patient person can lack ambition, the ability to go after what they desire. Lack of ambition does not mean a person is living contrary to the Spirit since the Spirit is guiding the person to a life of spiritual wholeness, contentment, and service.

Goodness

Goodness seems to be undervalued in the business world. Honesty, truthfulness, faithfulness, and fairness are qualities of goodness. Honestly is intrinsic to goodness and goodness is necessary for exemplary character development. One must be of good character to model the moral correctness that Paul describes. Goodness comes from the heart. Luke 4:45 reads, "The good man out of the good treasure of his heart brings forth what is good; and the evil *man* out of the evil *treasure* brings forth what is evil; for his mouth speaks from that which fills his heart" (Luke 4:45). The author suggests that goodness is a byproduct of a good heart. Luke also wrote, "For there is no good tree which produces bad fruit, nor, on the other hand, a bad tree which produces good fruit. For each tree is known by its own fruit. For men do not gather figs from thorns, nor do they pick grapes from a briar bush" (Luke 6:43).

Paul describes in the paragraph before his discourse on good fruit a list of bad habits. We could assume that goodness is the exact opposite of the list of sins. Or we could assume God is good and whatever God does is good. The simple way of approaching goodness would be to research what Jesus did and do that. A popular notion a few years ago was, "What would Jesus do?" While that is helpful, that is not enough since the Bible does not address every daily issue and social justice concern that we face in modern terms, but it is helpful in deciding how to augment what the Holy Spirit is doing to cultivate goodness in you.

The best fruit is produced when the Christian consistently tries to discern what the Spirit is doing and practices what will enhance the Spirit's work. The best fruit production requires perseverance on the part of the Christian. God can do the weeding, pruning, protecting, aerating, and fertilizing and provide the proper sunlight.

19

3
____

The Intersection

WHERE DO HIGH EMOTIONAL intelligence and the fruit of the Spirit link? Both require full participation by the person who fully seeks to improve their ability to manage life's challenges and win as a leader and as a person. Both involve character development. Both are within the individual's ability to affect. One supports the other and increases one's potential to win at life.

While it is possible to be a good person without making a concerted effort to increase emotional intelligence, the likelihood of becoming emotionally mature without effort is slim. Successful leaders are more than "good people" doing what they excel at doing.

Being a mature Christian requires action that includes engaging with the people and elements in their surroundings. Life has its frustrations which is why perseverance, also known as long-suffering, and self-control are so important for a person to master. For the Christian, the Holy Spirit is the higher power, and the enablement afforded to them by and through faith. Jesus, the central figure in Christian life, did not merely get by or rely only on his position of authority when he engaged with people. He taught about godly virtues and modeled them consistently for his followers. Christ did not act out of malice nor jealousy and responded to his critics without losing control. He was patient, especially with his disciples. He practiced spiritual discipline and showed compassion and empathy.

Mastery is key to spiritual development. Mastery over any bad habit, flaw, or foible takes effort and practice. While the Holy Spirit is at work, that work requires a response. We Christians use the term "born again" once a person becomes a believer. "Born" suggests that something new has occurred. Whether you are born naturally from your mother's womb, born again as a believer, or feel new after experiencing a traumatic event, some growing and learning needs to happen. God's part in the Christian's transformation is intentional and continuous. How fast, how intense, and how far he goes depends on the Christian's response.

God will show the Christian what characteristics he wants to cultivate, though we can get an idea of what virtues needs polishing by considering the choices we make and whether we even consult God on matters of virtue when faced with difficult decisions. Those who seek spiritual maturity would do well to increase their emotional intelligence to enhance development. Christians gaining mastery over their emotions will have the potential to respond to how the Spirit is grooming in mature ways. In other words, practicing what will increase your EI helps in your ability to follow the leading of the Holy Spirit.

Some theologians have grouped these virtues:

- Spiritual practices   Love, joy, peace

- Social virtues   Patience, kindness, goodness.

- Self-conduct   Faithfulness, patience, perseverance, and self-control.

This grouping may seem random, yet they match with core characteristics of EI.

Let us compare the fruit of the Spirit with the characteristics of high emotional intelligence:

- EQ   Fruit the Spirit produces.

- Self-awareness   Peace, love, joy.

- Temperance   Self-Control, patience/perseverance.
- Self-Motivation   Patience/perseverance.
- Social Awareness   Kindness, goodness or gentleness, faithfulness.
- Empathy   Kindness, goodness or gentleness, faithfulness.

It is not enough to identify the competencies but also to process the need for change. Some things are easier to accept when there is an explanation of why they need to happen and some instructions or practical application. Learning what constitutes emotional "hijacking" and how to avoid it is beneficial. It is easier to "walk by the spirit" when you have examined, and have attempted to deal with, what emotions cause you to resist the way of the Spirit (God). Following the Spirit develops high emotional intelligence only if you practice what develops high EI. No emotional maturity is gained if you refuse to manage your emotions. God does not merely wave his hand and high emotional intelligence manifests. God is working to cultivate the fruit (Godly traits), and you are responsible for emotional management.

One might say all a Christian needs to do to make strides in walking in the Spirit is to ask God for help and expect the Holy Spirit to assist. Asking God to help when you are emotional or feeling an emotion coming on is a mature response. The first step in maturing is recognizing how you feel. The second step is recognizing you need assistance.

What I have observed when people are trying to overcome emotional barriers to success is that underlying causes are treated instead of symptoms. The question we should ask ourselves is from where do causes originate? It appears that causes are linked to at least these three things: conditioning or grooming, trauma or genetics. Conditioning is things like parenting, culture, generational strongholds, and environmental forces. Genetics—health issues, mental or physical, predisposition to problems. I recognize this is not an exhaustive list.

Conditioning, environment, and birth order play a role in our emotional development. Both my older and younger brothers exhibited genius early in childhood. There I was, stuck in the middle. As much as my mother repeatedly told me I was not average, I didn't believe her but instead saw myself as being in shallow end of the gene pool. Since I was the only girl and not good at either math or science, I wasn't expected to make exceptional strides in either subject. I was, though, expected to be a shrewd negotiator, having neither the benefit of being the physically strongest nor the youngest sibling.

Due to complicated family dynamics, life at times was challenging. I learned to manage myself and my emotions for stability and didn't have a choice when it came to mood management. My faith played a significant role in my being able to manage my challenges since I believed my higher power protected and guided me. Children sometimes act out when home is a challenging place to live. Though I did act out in third grade, I believed, by the time I was a teen, that I could mentally resist negative comments, control my outward expressions, and cling to what I wanted to believe about myself.

Television and video condition us also. Growing up in the 1960s I witnessed women, through television newscasts, publicly burning their bras in trash cans. Though my mother tried to explain what "good girls" do, I knew that a revolution was taking place and felt somehow connected to the women who were seeking independence and change.

Although there are negative effects to watching television, there are lessons to gain when viewing TV through the lens of self-improvement. Television sometimes portrays gangsters who possess empathy and self-control, have influence, and love their families. We like the stories where the gangsters with high emotional intelligence win and the notorious ones with the short tempers lose. Papa Pope in the television series *Scandal* shot the love of his life in the head, and though he loved her, he knew she would never be safe. He was hemmed in by his adversaries who tried to use his loved one to make him surrender. Pope knew he would fail in the future to protect her and himself. Since he was a godless man, he put his hope only in himself, and when he was faced with decision he made a desperate, costly, yet oddly compassionate move.

Characters in other TV shows display high emotional intelligence along with criminal activity. Those characters are usually high in the criminal hierarchy. Gus Fring is a character from the show *Breaking Bad*. Gus is quiet, charming, smart, and able to keep his composure when others were losing theirs. He was, by no means, a good person, yet I would consider him to have high emotional intelligence. In the hit series *Snowfall* the character Franklin never manages to master the anger and violence that we see in him at the beginning of the series. He loses everything, including his mind, in the end.

People with high self-control are viewed as more responsible and trustworthy that those without. People with criminal mentality may develop their EI, yet virtues like compassion that come from forgiveness, not so much. I have met people who saw themselves as nice people due to their being generous, friendly, self-composed, and likeable. They did not believe their notorious qualities made them "all that bad." The character Gus Fring, though self-composed, wanted revenge, and he got it. His inability to move on from past hurt cost him his life.

Then there are complications that sin produces. One can be a great leader yet have some sins that cause their relationships to veer off-course. It is reported that Rev. Dr. Martin Luther King had extramarital affairs. So many outstanding accomplishments from a man with high emotional intelligence. Dr. King exhibited high EI regarding self-control when it came to violence, yet the Holy Spirit was hemmed in by Dr. King's lack of faithfulness. We all have our shortcomings and sins to bare, yet God is capable and willing to facilitate the change, so the "fruit" is produced and serves as evidence a person is winning spiritually.

Let's not forget the book of proverbial wisdom speaks to mood management. Proverbs 14:29–30 explains, "He who is slow to anger has great understanding, But he who is quick-tempered exalts folly. A tranquil heart is life to the body . . ."(Prov 14:29–30).

Accounts of people in the Bible give us a picture of them attempting to overcome the same things we deal with. Samson lacked impulse control, Naomi and Jeremiah struggled with depression, Noah managed his mood with alcohol, and King David was bored. Yet we also see Jonathan's love, Jesus' selflessness and empathy, Ruth's faithfulness and compassion, Job's suffering and perseverance. and Abigail's mature leadership.

The Bible speaks of God's moods also. There are descriptions of him as angry, moved with compassion, giving love, and in a creative mood when he formed the earth. God was intentional when he gave man emotions. Mood springs from emotions. In Exod 4:21 it is written that the LORD said to Moses of Pharaoh, "but I will harden his heart," giving support to the belief that emotions have a role in God's plan for humanity (Exod 4:2).

Mood has a lot to do with all aspects of emotions. Anxiety is discussed in the Bible, so clearly spiritual oneness includes dealing with bad moods. Philippians 4:6 is about mood, faith, and God's role in changing mood: "Be anxious for nothing, but in everything by prayer and supplication with thanksgiving let your requests be made known to God." Anxiety is fear. God wants Christians to trust him and to not let fear rob us of what we can have and accomplish. Joshua 1:9 reads, "Have I not commanded you? Be strong and courageous! Do not tremble or be dismayed, for the LORD your God is with you wherever you go" (Josh 1:9).

I have watched athletes leave or be stripped of lucrative deals because they could not control their emotions. Some fight with coaches, disregard rules, and have bad work ethics. What is often written off as just a bad attitude is often a symptom of something much larger. Fortunately, what leads to high IE can be learned. My dad was the first person to open my eyes to how other people could affect my future by just agitating me at the wrong time. He said to me when I was a teenager that if someone wants your job all they must do is try making you lose control in front of the boss or a customer.

At the 2022 Oscar awards ceremony, Will Smith made the bad decision to slap Chris Rock on national television. While it is understandable that some jokes cut to the core, violence was not the correct response. Will had a lot riding on his reputation as an artist and role model. Once he used violence, he proved he was emotionally immature. His emotions hijacked his thinking and his response to offense costs him in many ways including his relationship with fellow comedian Chris.

Relationship management is an element of emotional intelligence. "The works of the flesh destroy unity and community, while the fruit of the Spirit promotes corporate well-being. The Spirit empowers believers to seek what is right both in their relationship with God and in their relationships with people."[1] Paul's exhaustive list provides a guide for getting along with other people. The experience between Will and Chris should have caused us as a nation to examine our response to offense and our ability to control our emotions. Both men are comedians and are probably aware that some jokes hurt. Have we become too thin-skinned as a people, or have we just given ourselves permission to behave badly when we're feeling emotional because violence has become an acceptable way to deal with what or whom we don't like?

In the biblical account of Cain and Abel is an account of how the lack of self-control led to destruction. The story unfolds as two brothers brought their individual offers to God: "Abel, on his part also brought *an offering*, from the firstborn of his flock and from their fat portions. And the LORD had regard for Abel and his offering; but for Cain and his offering He had no regard. So, Cain became very angry and his face was gloomy. Then the LORD said to Cain, 'Why are you angry? And why is your face gloomy? If you do well, will *your face* not be cheerful? And if you do not do well, sin is lurking at the door; and its desire is for you, but you must master it.'" Cain talked to his brother Abel, and it happened that when they were in the field Cain rose up against his brother Abel and killed him (Gen 4:4).

God's disregard for Cain's offering put him in a bad mood. Anger is an emotion that can lead to destruction if unchecked, and God told Cain he must master it. We must master our emotions so

1. Braxton, *Galatians*, 344

that we are not drawn into regrettable behavior. I have seen, in the news, the same kind of response from people with low emotional intelligence. I have seen this response from people who have low resistance to sin. Cain could have resorted to cognitive reframing, picturing a difference for future offerings. God did warn him and offered Cain a perspective he could have embraced.

In the account of Ahab and Jezebel the same sort of jealousy arose. King Ahab saw a vineyard that belonged to his neighbor Naboth. Ahab spoke with his neighbor and requested the neighbor give him the vineyard to plant vegetables. It was prime real estate for Ahab because of its proximity to his house. The neighbor refused Ahab's request to purchase or swap properties explaining the property was his inheritance from his father.

Ahab went home in a bad mood, lays down in his bed and sulks. As bad moods often spread, his wife takes up the cause. She doesn't appreciate that her husband, the king, has been denied. The rest of the account unfolded this way: "So, she wrote letters in Ahab's name and sealed them with his seal and sent the letters to the elders and to the nobles who were living with Naboth in his city. Now she had written in the letters, saying, 'Proclaim a fast and seat Naboth at the head of the people; and seat two worthless men opposite him, and have them testify against him, saying, "You cursed God and the king." Then take him out and stone him to death'" (1 Kgs 21:8–10).

Ahab's low emotional control had a ripple effect. Unfortunately, his wife also had low emotional intelligence coupled with low morality. Due to low EI and no godly virtues, only bad fruit could be produced. Bad tree, bad fruit. The king and his wife built a house of evil and eventually met an untimely demise.

Jesus, on the other hand, is an example of someone with high emotional intelligence, while being the Holy Spirit personified. An example of self-control is Jesus in Luke 9:51: "When the days were approaching for His ascension, He was determined to go to Jerusalem; and He sent messengers on ahead of Him, and they went and entered a village of the Samaritans to make arrangements for Him. And they did not receive Him, because He was traveling toward

Jerusalem. When His disciples James and John saw this, they said, 'Lord, do You want us to command fire to come down from heaven and consume them?' But He turned and rebuked them. And they went on to another village." The disciples wanted revenge, but their leader commanded them to go another way. The disciples had the same gang mentality that exists today, yet their leader requested they not be led by their emotions but rather move on. His compassion and leadership reflected his emotional maturity. We can copy his efforts and behavior (Luke 9:51).

Having high emotional intelligence means we are in control of our futures and will continually seek to master our emotions. This does not mean we Christians should live our lives like unemotional robots. It means that we practice self-control, patience, cognitive re-framing, and empathy to live more fully in the freedom our salvation affords us.

High emotional intelligence includes self-motivation. To help motivate yourself, create an image that reminds you of where you are trying to go or how you need to grow. I'm not advocating for getting a tattoo, but create an image and display it somewhere you will regularly see it. For some it may be the sign of the cross; for others it may be something original. Constantine added the Chi-Rho christogram to his banner and made his men wear it on their helmets. His motto was "by this you shall conquer."[2]

Some emotions we can easily master as we mature. Some negative emotions may remain chained in the basement of our minds and growl when we're triggered. Either way we must decide who we want to be and how closely we want to adhere to Paul's list. We need to decide what is at risk if we don't. There is an apple tree that hangs over my backyard. It is my neighbor's tree, though I have tried to tend to it over the years, even praying over it during years it produced no fruit. Unfortunately, my neighbor has never tended to the tree, and half of it has several large dead branches. The other half of the tree is producing a few apples. It reminds me of what happens when we neglect things important for growth and maintenance.

2. Strauss, *Ten Caesars*, 295.

The Bible also speaks of social awareness in Colossians, chapter 4: "Conduct yourselves with wisdom toward outsiders, making the most of the opportunity. Let your speech always be with grace, *as though* seasoned with salt, so that you will know how you should respond to each person" (Col 4:5).

In the Christian faith a certain amount of suffering is expected. Paul writes, "we are afflicted in every way, but not crushed; perplexed, but not despairing; persecuted, but not forsaken; struck down, but not destroyed; always carrying about in the body the dying of Jesus, so that the life of Jesus also may be manifested in our body" (2 Cor 4:8–10). Paul also writes that we are overcomers, indicating that suffering is temporary and we can endure it. Perseverance, patience—also known as long-suffering—endurance and self-control are essential to walking in the spirit during times of suffering. Yet we are required to live our lives with godly virtues, faith and hope. "Hope, modern researchers are finding, does more than offer a bit of solace amid affliction; it plays a surprisingly potent role in life, offering an advantage in realms as diverse as school achievement and bearing up in onerous jobs. Hope in a technical sense, is more than the sunny view that everything will turn out right."[3] Paul writes, "Faith is the substance of things hoped for, the evidence of things unseen" (Heb 11:1).

The Christian Bible supports good mood management and holds insight into how our emotions impact our lives. Proverbial wisdom, the book of Proverbs, provides biblical truths that speak to the impact of high and low emotional intelligence. Below are some examples.

> Proverbs 17:22—A happy heart is good medicine, *and* a joyful mind causes healing, But a broken spirit dries up the bones.

> Proverbs 12:16—The [arrogant] fool's anger is quickly known [because he lacks self-control and common sense], but a prudent man ignores an insult.

---

3. Goleman, *Emotional Intelligence*, 87.

Proverbs 17:27 He who has knowledge restrains *and* is careful with his words, And a man of understanding *and* wisdom has a cool spirit [self-control, an even temper].

Proverbs 14:8 The wisdom of the sensible is to understand his way, but the foolishness of [shortsighted] fools is deceit.

4

What Will Happen If You Increase Your EI?

"Finally, brothers *and sisters*, whatever is true, whatever is honorable, whatever is right, whatever is pure, whatever is lovely, whatever is commendable, if there is any excellence and if anything worthy of praise, think about these things"(Phil 4:8).

Daniel Goleman asked the question, "Does our biology fix our emotional destiny, or can even an innately shy child grow into a more confident adult?"[1] If God is at work in the believer, then the answer is no, our biology does not determine our emotional destiny. Our willingness to let the work of the Spirit continue means change will occur and our progress will be continual. There are a variety of important effects increasing your EI will have on your life and spiritual development. The following is a list of effects.

If you increase your EI you will be less likely to engage in cancel culture. You will be better able to recognize when someone is not capable of being there for you when you experience challenges. People you believe you need may be experiencing their own

1. Goleman, *Emotional Intelligence*, 191.

challenges, and they may not share that information with you. Also, your situation could be triggering them, or they may not know what to do for you, so they distance themselves. You may be better able to realize their lack of a response or assistance does not mean the person doesn't care about you or is purposely avoiding you.

You become a better student/leader. People with high emotional intelligence make great students. It is less of a struggle to teach mature students than to teach impatient students with unrealistic expectations. Elisha, the prophet and a student of Elijah in the Bible, exhibited high emotional intelligence. He walked with and served his teacher for many years. You will notice in martial arts-themed movies that students who serve the master consistently become the hero of the story. The students that are impatient meet a less desirable fate. In the account of Elijah and Elisha we see how the student serves his master prophet with devotion and faithfulness. When Elijah's time ended Elisha went on to do great feats for God, modeling the same virtues his mentor modeled for him.

A professor I had in seminary told our class that in her experience the B+ student made the best ministry leaders. She said the A student typically possessed high academic acumen which did not always translate to success in leading other people. Ministerial leadership requires passion and dedication, love, and commitment. Not that a seminary student with high academic ability lacks those traits, the professor explained, but the seminary student with the B+ academic ability most often possessed a heart for people and other skills necessary for pastoral care. Ministerial leadership requires discernment, and not every person who knows that is willing to use it. It can be easier to ignore people and problems than to discern what's needed during engagements with parishioners and staff.

Increasing your EI gives the Holy Spirit the most to work with. My pastoral assignments have provided me with occasions to witness transformation. I have learned that your quality of life is dictated, in the long run, by your commitment to your spiritual and emotional self-management. The Holy Spirit is actively working during our whole lives since Christlikeness is a lifetime transformation. How fast and how much we are transformed depends on how much leeway we give to what the Spirit is doing. The "testing of our faith" is ongoing. Our experiences with God are ongoing. It takes a lifetime to discover every facet of God as he is a multifaceted being. Each encounter requires a new perspective gained through new challenges. New challenges provide new opportunities to grow and improve.

Endeavoring to increase your EI shows your willingness to invest in yourself. Increasing your EI shows your commitment to your own spiritual and professional development. You are worth your own time and energy. Believe in yourself. Believe you are worth the investment.

Increasing your EI is an act of obedience. By doing so you line up with what God wants to develop in you anyway: self-control, patience, kindness, empathy . . . God doesn't drop patience from the sky; it must be produced. Trials and challenges produce patience. Your response will be dictated by your emotional intelligence. If you grow spiritually and emotionally, then your response to challenges will likely be more mature, thereby promoting inner peace, something God desires for you.

High emotional intelligence increases your ability to influence others in a positive way, as an influencer and a role model. In ministry those whom you lead will do what you do and expect you will adhere to your Christian virtues while teaching, training, and mentoring them.

High EI affects your ability to serve others due to an increase in empathy, social awareness, and confidence. Jesus modeled high emotional intelligence for his followers. A storm arose while he and his disciples were on a boat. They awakened him from sleep and asked him why he seemed to not care they were distressed. He asked them why they were distressed and encouraged them to have faith. He calmed the fears of other people often during his ministry, and his followers learned to trust him.

High EI makes you less prone to sin. Paul directs us to "think on these things" (Phil 4:8) as, among other things, a way to stay out of trouble. A mind focused on augmenting the work of the Spirit is concentrated on what will promote successful living rather than on the list of activities Paul describes as the antithesis of walking by the Spirit.

People with high EI are less likely to commit violent crime. A study by Ahmed Megreya, "Emotional Intelligence and Criminal Behavior," shows a relationship of types of crimes to EI. Participants in the study were offenders in prison as well as non-offenders. The five types of domains used in the study were Intrapersonal Intelligence, Interpersonal Intelligence, Stress Management, Adaptability, and General Mood. "Using large samples of offenders and well-matched control participants, large and strong deficits in EI were observed among offenders, and these impairments were more severe among the violent offenders." The study found that prisoners who committed murder had lower EI than those who had committed theft and drug dealing. Prisoners who had committed theft had higher EI than those who had committed both murder and drug dealing. One result was that EI correlates with criminal thinking. "Forensic intervention programs should therefore include EI training, especially for violent offenders."[2]

Increasing your EI improves your ability to function in stressful situations and work satisfaction. Boyatsiz and McKee note how "work is hijacked" when emotions lead, though the ability to manage one's emotions leads to clearer thinking. Increasing your EI can lead to being a better team player and relationship builder, recognizing triggers and thinking through remedies. Reframing, looking at a situation from a different perspective, is a valuable skill that helps you be more discerning and promotes overall emotional wellbeing.

The ability to control your impulses while your brain thinks things through makes you less likely to make regrettable decisions. Most people know when they are in a bad mood. Bad energy can set the mood in a room and spread. You can think of changing your mood as cleansing your palate during a multi-course meal. Reset your thinking before you move on to something else or join other people. The person with a high degree of social awareness

2. Megreya, "Emotional Intelligence," 4.

is likely to choose to change their mood for not only their own benefit but for the benefit of others.

Noland in his book *The Heart of the Artist* discusses the effect of EI on leadership and unity: "Resolving relational conflict in a biblical way plays a key role in maintaining team unity."[3] He cites as an example Paul's admonition to the two women in the church at Philippi. The two women weren't getting along so Paul requested the women work out their differences.

Increasing your EI will aid you in positively managing your relationships since relating to family members can be challenging. Personality clashes can lead to estrangement and deep emotional wounds. With high social awareness and the Holy Spirit's influence you are less likely to hurt someone emotionally. That doesn't mean you will always avoid hurting someone's feelings, but rather you will be aware of how what you say will impact them. It means you are more likely to not hit back when someone else is speaking to you from a place of anger or hurt.

Managing someone else's mood may not always be possible, but you can manage your own. One step to increasing your EI is to be willing to admit mistakes and apologize. Managing yourself well not only has the potential to improve your engagement with family, but you in turn become a greater asset to your community. Energy at home you take with you when you leave. Side note: never covet another person's spouse. You never know how much emotional management their partner does to get the spouse ready to engage with the world outside of home.

You can become a better leader. Empathy, compassion, and kindness make you a better relationship manager. There is a big difference between a manager (coach) and a cheerleader. Coaches are invested, while cheerleaders bring the hype. I have learned, as a pastor, that people respond when they believe your vision includes them and even more so when they can see you are genuinely invested in their success.

The Christian way is to hold to hope, have faith, and persevere. Faith alone is not enough for spiritual growth, and some action is

3. Noland, *Heart of the Artist*, 104.

required to optimize the Spirits work within us. The prophet Habakkuk saw the disastrous situation of his surroundings and asked God how long God would put up with it. He said in chapter 2 of the book of Habakkuk, "I will stand at my guard post and station myself on the watchtower; And I will keep watch to see what He will say to me, And how I may reply when I am reprimanded (Hab 2:1). He knew he would need some change of attitude when God responded, and he thought about it in advance of God's response. That is an example of high emotional intelligence, thinking about your part in the change you seek ahead of the change occurring. The change or growth may require an emotional or physical sacrifice on your part. Habakkuk was ready.

Unlike Habakkuk, the prophet Jonah resorted to sulking when change was needed. Sulking is a sign of low emotional intelligence, and it doesn't desist on its own. Some effort is needed to come from under that cloud of hurt, anger, disappointment or self-pity.

Once you begin to practice de-escalation as a way of increasing your EI, it will happen automatically. The escalation department was where I worked for an insurance company, and people who were transferred to me had problems that needed addressing. It took a while to learned to effectively assist customers that are not in the best mood after being transferred to me.

Recently, I automatically de-escalated a situation when talking to the company rep that took my call concerning an issue with my service order. The tone of her voice made me aware she was frustrated with my displeasure concerning how the process was unfolding. My customer service training kicked in, and I took over the call. After changing my tone with her, I had pleasant conversation while she researched my issue. After assuring her I wasn't blaming her for the debacle created by her coworker, I apologized if I made her feel that way. Her voice softened, and she did her best to remedy the situation.

Increasing your emotional intelligence may cause other Christians to praise God. Sometimes we don't really listen to what people in our lives are saying about habits and foibles that need addressing. Our friends, coworkers, and loved ones, for example, may be praying we change or at least to better manage the emotions that keep us at odds with them. I had a supervisor who was difficult to engage with, especially when we needed her assistance. She was moody and at time downright mean. My other coworker would tell me how she prayed and practiced spiritual discipline every morning just to be able to engage with the supervisor. One day, during an informal team gathering, the supervisor said she was working at being a better communicator because she recognized she needed to take care in how she spoke to us. After hearing her confession my spirits lifted, and I praised God.

The company you keep may not accept who you are endeavoring to be. Some may want you to stay the same since change may mean they will no longer be able to relate to you or you may no longer need them. I had a childhood friend who became upset and moody whenever I learned or attempted something new. My growth somehow caused her anxiety, and she responded by making rude remarks and/or distancing herself. Persevere despite what others accept. You may suffer for it, but seek change for the sake of growth, wellbeing, and a closer relationship with God. Apostle Peter explains, "But even if you should suffer for the sake of righteousness, you are blessed. And do not fear their intimidation, and do not be troubled" (1 Pet 3:14). The author implores us to be courageous and conduct ourselves according to the virtues the Holy Spirit is cultivating. He explains that is better to be slandered for your display of high emotional intelligence than to be judged for a bad or immature response to persecution.

5

Leadership

"The Lord's bond-servant must not be quarrelsome, but be kind to all, able to teach, patient when wronged, with gentleness correcting those who are in opposition, if perhaps God may grant them repentance leading to the knowledge of the truth" (2 Tim 2:24–25).

A note on Talent Smart's website reads "Decades of research point to emotional intelligence (EQ) as the critical factor that sets star performers apart from the rest of the pack."[1] The VIA home page reads, "Research shows that understanding and applying your strengths boost confidence, increase happiness, strengthen relationships, manage problems, reduce stress, accomplish goals, build meaning and purpose, and improve work performance."[2] These two widely known institutions extol the benefits of personal development. Both character development and high emotional intelligence link in no greater place than leadership development.

Boyatzis and McKee wrote this of leaders with high emotional intelligence: "Great leaders face the uncertainty of today's world with hope: they inspire through clarity of vision, optimism,

1. TalentSmart.
2. Via Institute on Character.

and a profound belief in their—and their people's—ability to turn dreams into reality. Great leaders face sacrifice, difficulties, and challenges as well as opportunities, with empathy and compassion for the people they lead and those they serve."[3]

Montaudon-Tomas writes, "Spiritual values are encouraged by integrity, by doing what is right, by making business decisions based on the principles of God, which include righteousness, truth, honesty and excellence. Exemplary organizations aim to honor God, and their pursuit of excellence transforms lives through a clear commitment to its people, fair compensation, performance recognition, and growth opportunities, bringing about the best in their collaborators. Even if some employees do not share the same faith in an organization, everyone is treated with dignity and respect."[4]

Great leaders are the catalyst of the organization. Spiritual values can and should be encouraged by the "resonant leader." According to Boyatzis the resonant leader is not without their own values, characteristics, and leadership skills instrumental to high emotional intelligence. An organization cannot reach the level of exemplary status without "resonate leaders." Christian leaders, who take seriously Paul's admonition, must endeavor to raise their emotional intelligence, thereby increasing their ability to model spiritual values while assisting the organization in reaching its potential. Leaders must be confident rather than insecure, know who they are, and know how life challenges affect them.

Skills that promote and encourage spiritual values of others are empathy, organizational awareness, transparency, and honesty. Virtues that bring out the best in others are empathy, self-control, patience, goodness, and faithfulness. As the leader goes, so goes the organization. Leaders with high emotional intelligence can seek to minimize employee resentment derived from poor employee engagement. Emotionally immature leaders jeopardize employee wellbeing, job security, and productivity.

In my early twenties I worked in a shop managed by a supervisor with high emotional intelligence. Periodically, each day, Bob

3. Boyatzis and McKee, *Resonant Leadership*, 3.

4. Montaudon-Tomas, *Avoiding Spiritual Bankruptcy*, 19.

took a few minutes to look around a large room full of people and machinery and take mental inventory of everyone's activity. Very little employee activity ever escaped his assessment. He was personable, trustworthy, loyal, and unafraid to take actions necessary to ensure productivity remained high. He knew our names, our spouse's names, and the names of our kids. He was what football analysis called "unflappable." His ability to control himself and manage his engagement with shop employees was admirable.

Some years later, I worked for a nonprofit agency in a department led by a manager who, unlike Bob, was very temperamental. Once Dave closed his office door, we who worked with him knew to avoid asking him any questions. Our need for counsel with him was met with either silence, indifference, and/or snide remarks. After his bad mood changed he questioned us about why we would make decisions without his consent. At times he accused me of not following protocol when there was no protocol to follow. Since obtaining his sign off on a project wasn't an option during his bad mood days, I made the wisest decisions I could make, even though I knew there would be negative consequences.

During my tenure with the organization, Dave never appeared to realize how his behavior affected other employees. His low self-awareness and self-management affected morale and productivity. "From self-awareness—understanding one's emotions and being clear about one's purpose—flows self-management, the focused drive that all leaders need to achieve their goals. Without knowing what we're feeling, we're at a loss to manage those feelings. Instead, our emotions control us."[5] Not only did Dave's emotions control him but Dave's constantly changing goals left his staff confused and off-balance.

Having been a pastor for several years I know well the benefits of high emotional intelligence and owe a lot of my success to my ability to control my emotions, empathize with others, and motivate myself when feeling unappreciated. My ability to bond with others, quickly establish rapport, and move people to action served me well. Unlike in the cooperate world, leading a voluntary

5. Goleman, Boyatzis, and McKee, *Primal Leadership*, 45.

association is without the carrot of high wages. Most church lay leaders, especially in congregations of less than 250 members, are not paid. In some congregations only the pastor is paid and sometimes not very well.

Leading a non-profit has not only the challenges that corporate leaders face, but culture can drive the organization in ways that may be politically correct but inefficient. Nowhere is that more prevalent than in religious organizations. Members with the potential to make large donations may make demands that do not follow protocol, organizational bylaws, or good common sense. In addition, pastors have close relationships with members and staff who are often also members. Pastors are often involved in members' lives, and counseling is often part of the job description. I have observed some religious leaders employing methods to avoid engagement with members, such as remaining as distant and as unapproachable as possible, preaching or teaching doctrine that is controlling, or being emotionally abusive, deflecting or blaming people for their own problems.

Peter writes that Jesus was the quintessential leader of a voluntary organization who possessed outstanding virtue (1 Pet 2:21). Jesus set the standard for high emotional intelligence. His characteristics serve as the model for what Paul describes as the fruit of the Spirit. In Luke chapter 9, Jesus' disciples went into a city where the residents refused Jesus. The disciples were offended and so much so, they asked Jesus if they should seek the city's destruction. "But He turned and rebuked them, and said, "You do not know what kind of spirit you are of" (Luke 9). Jesus reminded them of who they were, was not influenced by their mood, then took them a different way, thereby modeling high emotional intelligence for his followers. He wasn't angry or offended but instead got their attention of his followers, averted violence, and chose another route.

These days I observe some of my colleagues in pastoral ministry struggle due to low emotional intelligence. Criticism, offense, poor counseling, and communication skills were part of the problem, as well as disappointment with salary and no real friendships.

One of the leading causes of people leaving ministry is difficult people. Most ministers new to being a pastor are ill-equipped to deal with the variety of personalities and situations that arise between members. The offering of leadership development workshops for ministers are multiple yet very few, if any, address EI. Make EI a part of leadership development for clergy.

There is an upside to being a pastor and there are opportunities for growth. Pastors can take advantage of opportunities to assess from where member habits and traits originate. The office of the pastor provides an excellent vantage point from where to view family dynamics and determine root causes for certain patterns of behavior. To increase their EI they should consider their own pattern of thinking and family dynamics to better understand others.

Another means to higher EI for a pastor is to establish resonance with elderly members. Older members can be your greatest resource if you make them feel you care about them. Older people like to talk about the past, and their salvation stories can shine a light on their thinking and behavior. Ask their advice, and don't rush them. Here is where gentleness, kindness, and perseverance come in, and it may take time to win a few of them over.

When it comes to ministry, longevity does not necessarily indicate winning and does not equal success. A study done by Pew Research on pastors reports that when asked, a large percentage of pastors reported if they had to do things over, they would have chosen some other occupation. Pastors with the highest job satisfaction are the ones who have learned how to how to lead, rest, love, manage their family dynamics, and have mastered operating with high emotional intelligence. "Love has been considered as the cornerstone of servant leadership, and organizational effectiveness and has been associated to doing the right things at the right time for the right reasons."[6]

Though being a pastor has its challenges, I have met pastors who are really winning at leading. All of them show evidence that the Holy Spirit is producing an abundance of the best fruit. Fortunately, for me, the church I pastored paid for my continuing

6. Crowther, *Fruit of the Spirit*, 24

education, and I was able to earn an Emotional Intelligence Leader certificate from Case Western Reserve University that benefited the church as well as myself.

If I had to do my past over again, I still would choose pastoral ministry. I appreciate every patient ministry leader that mentored me. "Patience is a virtue" is not just a cliché. Impatience not only affects others but tends to be contagious. Microwaves and "get it same day" promises encourage impatience, and it causes anxiety for leaders as well as for those whom they lead. It can also cause people to feel insecure about meeting expectations and following directions. Impatience, most often, arises out of fear. Fear of not meeting deadlines, fear of losing ground, fear of losing money, fear our health won't hold up in the future. Leaders should often ask themselves what is driving their impatience and write it down. Keeping a journal can help uncover underlying causes for impatience and anxiety.

The apostle Paul was himself a patient leader, and oftentimes he was misunderstood. He sat in prison on several occasions and patiently waited for his circumstances to change. He had the patience to write letters to congregations and engage in constant prayer for their benefit. Paul understood the human condition and was very patient and empathetic yet did not tolerate folly. Paul understood people, was transparent about his own past and shortcomings, and advised congregants to be patient with each other, knowing change takes time.

With young people turning away from traditional church it is imperative that church leaders have high EI, be willing to be transparent, and be able to articulate vision in such a way that young people can get excited. There is no shortage of new ministries, which is a good thing. What is problematic is that ministry creators often are on their own and lack the necessary people skills that help them to solicit support.

New churches are often started by people who left a church due to offense. The problem is if emotions, like offense, are the motivation for creating something new, that negative mindset will dictate how the creator will move forward with managing relationships needed for support. If the creator takes seriously Paul's command to obtain the virtues that will bring about spiritual fulfillment, they will have the right formula to build "resonant" relationships. Engaging in emotional exercises that increase their emotional intelligence will also help them augment the work of the Spirit.

Being a leader with high EI means being able to manage your own disappointments. After graduating from seminary with my DMin, I was disappointed with not being able to obtain a teaching assignment. While working on obtaining my doctorate, I spent considerable time and energy exploring a concept that I believed had considerable merit and was eager to share information about it with others. After a few days of sulking, I realized there were other ways to disseminate information and engage my community. I created a symposium and invited other seminary graduates to participate by sharing their dissertations with seminary students and the church community. After I received sponsorship that covered the cost of the speaker and a workshop leader, I forgot about being disappointed. Disappointment turned to excitement and discovery. Not only did the symposium go on as planned, it continued for years after that.

Love, self-sacrifice, service, and kindness Paul extols as the Christian way. Yet the expectations of the people who pay our salaries may not align with those virtues. Where does that leave the leader? It leaves the leader to consider their values and to decide who they want to be rather than who someone else wants them to be. The Holy Spirit is at work, and in order to grow, Christians need to give way to what the spirit is doing. Thus love, compassion, and kindness shouldn't be squelched because it will inhibit the work of the Spirit.

Leading with love and empathy does not mean you will avoid stress. Boyatzis and McKee wrote, "The unique demands of leadership typically trigger a pattern of power stress and the Sacrifice Syndrome. In resonant leaders, this destructive combination is transformed by engaging certain specific experiences—such as mindfulness, hope, and compassion—that result in renewal.[7] The authors go on to say that damage that results in "unbalanced or unchecked behavior in leadership" manifests in burnout, illnesses, fatigue, and restlessness.[8]

Leaders who fail to admonish in love cause resentment which can often spawn passive aggressive behavior, not to mention unwanted attrition. Loving means giving up selfish desires. Managers who sacrifice everything and everyone else on the altar of selfish desire end up alone. Spiritual leaders' marriages that fail are often a result of self-centeredness. Corporate executives' marriages fail for the same reason as well as other stresses and time demands. "Awakening to one's spiritual values and one's source of hope and renewal are of paramount importance to becoming a visionary leader whose skills and character join hands. It is an example of emotional intelligence vocationally focused."[9]

We Christian leaders need to decide what's important. Leading from a place of love, compassion, peace, goodness, and joy may be seen as a sign of weakness in some arenas. Yet humility does not mean weak, and joy does not mean we ignore what is going on around us. It means we choose to be different as disciples of Christ. That does and will produce some tension, and it should. Some jobs require you to finesse the system for some processes to flow properly. Progress may require actions that clash with your values. For instance, I worked for a company that required reps to complete scripts. On multiple occasions the rep was faced with choosing answers on the script that did not actually match with the conversation they had with the customer. The supervisor, in charge of training, instructed reps to just choose the answer that would make the process flow properly.

I knew from experience that making such a request puts a person on a slippery slope in regard to honesty and trust worthiness. When is an answer a lie, and when is it just doing what is requested and expected? Also, it is a matter of influence. You're

7. Boyatzis and McKee, *Resonant Leadership*, 205.

8. Boyatzis and McKee, *Resonant Leadership*, 210.

9. Ott, *Emotional Intelligence*, 20.

the one leading, guiding, and practicing social awareness. Telling someone to choose an option that does not reflect the truth can, at the very least, bring some discomfort to your inner peace, and it should. Never be fully comfortable with lying, yet we make decisions and move on since great leaders don't become burdened by past decisions. If you constantly do, it may be a signal to find another job.

Unrealistic expectations of the people you lead can trigger frustration. Some years ago I explained to the church volunteers a vision God had given to me. My creativity was in overdrive, and I was excited about bringing God's vision for an interactive dinner to fruition. Things didn't go as planned. As the event unfolded on the scheduled date, I tried to mask how disappointed I was that people weren't following directions. The actors were not on cue, kids were disorganized, timing was an issue. I thought to myself, "How could they mess this up? Wasn't I clear enough?" And I even reviewed the instructions given to try to identify what went wrong. Later, a member remarked that I was not the easiest person to please. She was laughing while explaining a previous debacle, and I felt bad about causing her stress. She said, "I could see in your eyes that we were ruining your vision." That made me feel even worse. Another person came to me and talked about how much their guest enjoyed the festivities. The kids that were involved had a great time. I realized that how things look in my head is not necessarily how God's plan comes together. The kids having great time or the visitor's view of God's people in action may have been God's sole purpose for the occasion.

That incident inspired me to be more aware of how I made people feel, especially when I find myself obsessing over what I desire to accomplish. I'm still driven but I am much more aware of my expectations of other people. There is an account in the Bible of a family that invited Jesus to dinner. While sister Martha set about preparing dinner for the many invited guests, the other sister, Mary, stopped working and sat at Jesus' feet to listen to his wisdom. Martha became upset with her sister for not helping. Jesus told Martha that Mary had chosen the more excellent way.

While I do believe that if I were Martha, I would have been upset with Mary, I do get the point. Not only was Jesus saying to choose what is spiritually important; he was saying to have patience when it comes to what is important to other people.

Paul included patience in the list of virtues not only because it is key to finding inner peace but because having patience is one way to express love. Martha, no doubt, loved her sister, yet her priority was in the service. Martha's social awareness was limited when it came to what was important to her sister, yet Martha's service should not be ignored since service is a byproduct of social awareness. The expectation of women in that day and time, along with other cultural influences, was partly to blame for her reaction to Mary's not assisting, and she probably followed protocol by appealing to an authority figure, Jesus. Jesus modeled patience and compassion for both women and explained to Martha how she could obtain peace if she worried less.

How do we groom future leaders? Lead by example and be an approachable role model. Paul modeled walking in the Spirit and modeled leadership for his mentees. We should teach what we know even when we struggle with personal and spiritual growth. When it comes to children, don't take for granted that emotional intelligence is being practiced in their homes. Take opportunities to teach what worked and didn't work for you as a child.

High EI is crucial to good health and longevity, especially in this time where young adults are demanded more in return for their company loyalty. Great leaders sacrifice, practice mindfulness, and have confidence in themselves and others. Great leaders give others room and motivation to be successful. Great leaders attempt to understand and empathize with the people they lead. The expectation of leaders can become overwhelming, which makes it important to take time off to rest, have fun, reconnect with loved ones, and tend to our emotional needs.

6

Community

"The best use of life is love. The best expression of love is time. The best time to love is now" (Rick Warren).

THE OXFORD DICTIONARY DEFINITION of community: "a group of people living in the same place or having a particular characteristic in common."[1] Jesus said everyone around us is a neighbor; therefore, our neighbors make up our community. Our communities are in dire need of leaders and community members with high emotional intelligence due to corrosion of our supporting institutions. Whether the communities are churches, schools, neighborhoods, cities, or families.

If Paul wrote this letter in the context of community, who benefits when a person or people seek to increase their EI? The answer is "his neighbor," hence all the community, whether their community is a religious institution, neighborhood business, voluntary association, or workplace. History and studies have shown that as the leader goes, so goes the organization they lead, since an organization's aura reflects that of the leader. High emotional intelligence of the leader can impact the community in a positive way

1. "Community."

and be contagious. Leaders influence the community's temperature, whether the leaders are teachers, coaches, pastors, parents or presidents of countries.

God has created us to be social beings rather than isolated. Individuals with high EI have the potential to positively influence in the realm in which they operate. Brad R. Braxton explains Paul's words this way: "The works of the flesh destroy unity and community, while the fruit of the Spirit promotes corporate well-being."[2] He goes on to say, "Spiritual people do not retreat from 'the world' in order to avoid moral contamination. Rather, the Holy Spirit compels believers to engage the world with the hopes of returning it to holiness and wholeness."

High EI augments the work of the Spirit. Let us look at what is required of us in community with others.

Hebrews 12:14 says, "Pursue peace with all people, and the holiness without which no one will see the Lord" (Heb 12:14). Passing the peace in church settings means to share the peace of Christ with other members. Why not pass the peace in our communities? We do it by being neighborly and by purposeful engagement including pursuing justice. The apostle James advises us to do just that. "What use is it, my brothers *and sisters*, if someone says he has faith, but he has no works? Can that faith save him? If a brother or sister is without clothing and in need of daily food, and one of you says to them, 'Go in peace, be warmed and be filled,' yet you do not give them what is necessary for *their* body, what use is that? In the same way, faith also, if it has no works, is dead, *being by itself*" (Jas 2:14–17).

Outward peace for good community engagement requires self-control. Our communities in the US have increasingly become more violent. Dr. Martin Luther King wrote, "Violent persons surrender themselves to powerlessness as they promote un-redemptive suffering and thus capitulate to history—the killing fields of yesterday. Nonviolent persons, however, surrender themselves to the only true power there is as they promote redemptive suffering and thus capitulate to the future—the life-enhancing fields of

2. Braxton, "Galatians," 344.

tomorrow." King declared, "We still have a choice today: nonviolent coexistence or violent co-annihilation."[3]

Leading voices in EI are unanimous in reporting that a way to increase EI is to be okay with not always winning a point in a conversation or always proving to be right. That is one way to promote peace, both within and with others. Self-confidence, rather than the arrogance our egos produce, generates peace, promotes unity, and spiritual bonding.

Patience in the context of community means waiting with no expectation of return, on the time spent, from the community itself. If long-suffering or patience is to be achieved, we must be able to do more than just waiting until difficult people leave our presence. I believe the value of patience is what God is cultivating in the individual.

Mature, purposeful, successful engagement within a community also requires high self-awareness, self-management and social competencies. There is a higher expectation of Christians when it comes to engagement, or at least there use to be. The very definition of Christianity includes following a model that leads to our best self, which reflects the image of Christ. Christianity is as much a way of living as it is a religion. It is not so easy to be the hands and feet of Christ when you don't like people, look down on them, and/or have little regard for their needs. High social awareness in the context of spiritual bonding may not be so easy for some introverts to obtain.

Mood has everything to do with our ability to positively engage with others. The leader's mood sets the tone for work, worship services, family time, sporting events, meetings and any setting where collaboration takes place. The artistic leader's mood sets the tone for the music and aesthetics. God requires us to be cheerful givers, love others, honor our mothers and fathers, seek no revenge, forgive, practice hospitality, admonish and build each other up. Given the fruit that is being produced in the Christian, what is the appropriate mindset for engagement with other people

3. Young, *Self-Consciousness*, 70.

when they aren't in a good mood? High EI helps with our ability to appropriately respond to challenges Paul's commands present.

God does show Christians how they are viewed by others. Situations occur in community, and particularly church settings, that give us an indication of how others experience us. Some are even able to "hear" the voice of God during the encounters. Being cognizant of how others experience you is part of self-awareness.

LET US EXAMINE HOW TO WALK IN THE SPIRIT IN THE CONTEXT OF COMMUNITY

Love

Love can serve as the foundation for relationship building. Love may very well be the reason one seeks to be transformed, the motivation for self-improvement. Love just might be the rationale for community engagement. John 15:12 says, "This is My commandment, that you love one another, just as I have loved you (John 15: 12). Engagement presents an opportunity for us to show others we love them. Empathy and love can be the basis for engagement with understanding, though it isn't an easy task since some people are difficult to love. Yet the command to love one another is not optional; therefore, a change of heart is often required to engage with difficult people.

Understanding and empathy are crucial to genuine engagement. Understanding can lead to altruistic behavior. We see in the book of Acts Jesus' disciples encouraging sharing, caring, and "having all things in common". Community required some degree of altruism from its members. Altruism is something that can and should be developed. You can teach a person to be charitable, like mothers who teach their children to share. But true altruism, like emotional intelligence, is born out of our own desire to care and share. It is a virtue that the Holy Spirit will develop if a person gives way to what the Spirit wants to accomplish in cultivating the best fruit.

The Best Fruit

Empathy is not necessarily altruism, though it may be the motivation for altruistic behavior. Goleman suggests altruism increases with empathy. Altruism involves caring without expectation of personal gain. Some cultural groups may be seen as more altruistic than others. What some people fail to understand is that there is a correlation between identity and altruism. I did a survey in grad school that included alumni from a historically black college. The survey was created to gather information about why alumni supported the college's annual fund. On the survey I requested participants to identify their race. Although all but 3 participants were African American, the participants described themselves as Negro, Black, African American, Colored, and Mixed. What I discover was that the most philanthropic age group identified themselves as Negro. There is a good reason for that. Those who identified themselves as Negro were the people born during and just after the great depression that experienced community differently from their younger constituents. The great migration had unfolded during their lifetime. Economic conditions and safety had also dictated that people of color "stick together." The church, being the center of family activity, also taught altruism and linked it to being Christlike.

If we see ourselves as a work in progress, then altruism needs to be sought after, in addition to goodness, kindness, and love. What does this have to do with emotional intelligence? If what Goleman hypothesizes is correct, then the Holy Spirit will also cultivate altruism just like empathy and not only to the benefit of each Christian but to the benefit of those with whom Christians engage, i.e., the community. Altruism supported by kindness, for the believer, is the work of the Spirit.

Those who endeavor to walk in the spirit should practice what will increase their understanding, thereby augmenting the Spirits' efforts. Christians are also required to bear each other's burdens. How should we respond when people need us, who need intervention? Certainly not by firing Bible bullets and scaring them with strong-arm or politically motivated tactics. We must first understand them and their circumstances, and how they arrived. Movies or television shows that provide trilogies so that the viewer understands how the person came to be give the viewer a different perspective. We should learn from that. When we think we know what is best for others based solely on our experiences, we can easily disregard or make light of another person's pain, especially if their experience doesn't neatly fit into our theology.

Understanding can mean recognizing how poverty affects cognitive ability. Poverty is a condition rather than an emotion. Yet like emotions, scarcity can "hijack" the mind. Scarcity can and does affect your mood and your ability to make good decisions. Mullainathan and Shafir, in the book *Scarcity: The New Science of Having Less and How It Defines Our Lives*, theorize that "Scarcity is more than just the displeasure of having very little. It changes how we think. It imposes itself on your mind."[4] In light of that theory scarcity must affect emotional intelligence. Can we expect people who suffer from poverty, and particularly ones who are also malnourished, to make good decisions? How does this inform our understanding of the cycle of poverty as it relates to crime? What do we offer by way of help that is appropriate?

The authors wrote about scarcity as more than just the lack of food. They deal with emotional hijackings that relate to lack of time, good health, and other situations that affect a person's cognitive ability. We should address lack in our own lives to augment the work of the Spirit. God requires Christians to not only love but to bare one another's burdens. Yet if we are poor in spirit due to lack, how then can we help? One answer is to address our own lack of love, passion, and imagination when it comes to solving community problems.

How can the punishment fit the crime if the punishment has no restorative value based on our understanding of what the offender lacks emotionally? Paul offers in his letter to the Galatians, "Brethren, even if anyone is caught in any trespass, you who are spiritual, restore such a one in a spirit of gentleness; each one looking to yourself, so that you too will not be tempted" (Gal 6:1). That does not mean we, as a community, are soft on crime, since Paul was referring to the church. Yet we can take this as a lesson on

---

4. Mullainathan and Shafir, *Scarcity*, 7.

how to approach crime, restitution, and restorative justice, using wisdom and empathy that high emotional intelligence affords us. Part of the reason recidivism is high in the US is because the incarcerated person does not have a space in which to practice being better. In prison their highest priority is survival.

Where does diversity come in? Our churches are filled with people who are least somewhat like us. I heard Dr. King say in a speech that 11 am on Sunday is "our most segregated hour." Yet our neighborhoods, schools, and workplaces tend to be at least somewhat diverse. How does our emotional intelligence affect our ability to work, live, or manage in these places? We must at least manage to be civil. "Restoring civility asks of us sacrifice. Restoring civility, therefore, requires of us a commitment to moral and spiritual formation."[5]

"Using an ethnic slur reduces someone to a member of a class of people and, thereby, removes their individuality and inherent value. Insult is the refuge of those who do not fully understand why they believe what they believe or are anxious about the merits of their position. It also is the chosen tool of the lazy. Civility is not lazy."[6]

We can teach our family members the importance of high EI and explain that we may not be able to change the way people treat us, but we can manage our own emotions and possibly influence their perception. We can engage children in activities that produce confidence and support positive self-image. Teach children they can determine who they want to be and how to respond to challenges. Teach them how to engage with people in preparation for them becoming leaders and business owners. Going back to "temperament is not destiny." There are youths who are in the pipeline to prison. Someone needs to step up and teach them about emotional maturity and the benefits of high EI instead of using negative stimulation in hopes of producing positive results.

5. Kelsey, "Practicing Civility," 2.
6. Kelsey, "Practicing Civility," 5.

Goodness

Jesus' sacrifice at the cross is an example of goodness. It was a self-less act to the benefit of mankind. Scriptural support for kindness can be found in Micah 6:8: "He has told you, mortal one, what is good; And what does the Lord require of you, But to do justice, to love kindness, And to walk humbly with your God?" (Mic 6:8).

Joy of Serving

The term "community service" has taken on an all-new connotation. The justice system uses it to describe the making of restitution through community work, but it is more than that. During the prosperity movement people became more interested in seeking wealth and less interested in servicing their communities. These are a variety of other reasons Christians don't serve their community: too busy, don't like people, don't believe service is relevant, fear of other cultures, crime, fewer baby boomer volunteers due to aging, and not really having a heart for God's people. In other words, lack of engagement due to self-centeredness, aging, and fear. Hopefully we will find ways to reverse the trend and to share joy of the Spirit.

Patience

Hopefully raising our social awareness causes us to be better citizens in the realm of God. Being harsh with others does not usually produce the effect we want. Paul asks us to remember who we were before we became more mature. When I was a pastor, one of the challenges I swore would drive me to drinking was giving advice to someone who requested it, only for them to disregard the advice then come back for more advice. The way I chose to subvert those feeling of frustration is to remind myself I was once difficult, and yet God never abandoned me nor dealt with me unreasonably.

Pope Paul said, "Responsible citizenship is a virtue, and participation in political life is a moral obligation."[7] An attempt to enter politics as a way of bearing fruit for the good of the community might be best bolstered by high spiritual and emotional discipline. The ability to haggle, persuade, or verbally joust without losing your temper or perspective is imperative if one is to be successful in that arena. Any person attempting to be successful in a job or career that requires a high degree of discipline will do well to work on increasing their emotional intelligence as a way of avoiding being consumed by the challenges of their assignment.

As voters, choosing candidates wisely may impact our community in positive ways. Unfortunately, there are times when there is a void of candidates with high emotional intelligence. Choose leaders that understand that no good comes to any government that fails to tend to the welfare of all its citizens.

7. Pope Francis, *Joy of the Gospel*, 13.

7

Triggers

"We are destroying arguments and all arrogance raised against the knowledge of God, and we are taking every thought captive to the obedience of Christ" (2nd Cor 10:5).

THE JOB OF THE grower is to till, seed, water, cultivate, and harvest. How do they keep the pest off the fruit? What is the pest, and what is the treatment? Why were chemicals used when it appears a net would do? I once harvested grapes for a local winery, and the first thing we did was remove the nets that had been applied to keep birds from eating the fruit. Raising our emotional intelligence can help us gain the peace that can protect our mental health like the nets on the grapes. Rather than making drugs or alcohol (chemicals) our first choice to mood management, we can instead try meditation, exercise, or other remedies without negative aftereffects. Recognizing triggers is a useful tool for mood management and keeping emotional pests away.

Triggers can elicit mild emotions or a bad physical response. In my fifteen years as a pastor and thirty-five years of raising kids, I have seen a lot of emotional responses to situations, crises, people, and events. Medication, fragrances, and even sounds can trigger emotions. Also, weather can be triggering. Healthline reports, "Rapidly rising temperatures could trigger a mood episode, particularly for people with people with bipolar disorder." It also reports "warm, sunny weather may affect brainpower by boosting your memory, helping you feel more open to new information, improving inattentiveness, if you have ADHD."[1]

A trigger I struggled with while growing up was my being misunderstood by other people particularly when I shared my deepest thoughts. I didn't understand my calling and spiritual gifts made me unique and would one day enable me to minister successfully to others. My way of coping with misunderstanding was to withdraw and keep my thoughts to myself. Eventually I figure out that I could mentally block negative comments, hold tightly to my hopes and dreams and be ready to run straight into my destiny when the opportunity presented itself. A tweet from Morgan Richard Oliver explains what I couldn't then put into words "Letting people be wrong about you or a situation while keeping your peace and focus is the most misunderstood power move you will ever make."[2]

Experiences that bring us face to face with our weaknesses trigger emotions. Guilt, desire, or whatever makes you vulnerable can be triggering. We can want to do what is pleasing to God, yet the world offers much to the contrary. Paul said "For what I am doing, I do not understand; for I am not practicing what I would like to do but I am doing the very thing I hate. But if I do the very thing I do not want to do I agree with the Law, that the Law confessing is good" (Rom 7:15). In other words, we do the very thing that displeases God rather than live in the freedom our salvation affords us. Let's not delude ourselves. It isn't always easy to not sin, and Paul admits that. Yet we have the Holy Spirit and can draw on his power to resist. Paul also wrote, "for you were once darkness, but now you are light in the Lord; walk as children of light (for the fruit of the light consists in all goodness, righteousness, and truth), as you try to learn what is pleasing to the Lord (Eph 5:8).

1. "Yes, Weather Can Affect Mood and Energy."
2. Oliver, Twitter, May 18, 2022

Guilt, like desire, is an emotion and can be mastered. Mastery over sin is good for our emotional wellbeing. Let us put some energy into avoiding what makes us feel guilty in the first place. In the old days it was common for preachers to attempt to control people with fear. Fearmongering is the lowest form of control or influence. It is the antithesis of high emotional intelligence. Intelligent Christians need intelligent answers to life's challenges, including how to handle sin. Sin is described by Paul in the paragraph prior to his description of the fruit of the Spirit. So, our dilemma is not that we don't recognize sin but that our transformation includes what tests our faith, endurance, and our ability to make good decisions, thus avoiding sin.

Dealing with root or underlying causes of emotional challenges helps in our quest to increase our emotional intelligence and our attempt to avoid sin. I had a friend I'll call Alex. Alex grew up as the baby brother in his large family in the late 1940s. At the age of sixteen he went to live in New York with his older brothers. Without the guidance of his mother or any mother figure, he learned the way of the streets. The older brother enabled him, which supported Alex's wild lifestyle and desire to have whatever he wanted.

Alex was fascinated with guns, drugs, gambling, and street life, and he learned destructive behavior from the people he met. Alex became a selfish, self-centered adult with low impulse control. To support his gambling addiction, he turned to bank robbery. Alex eventually landed in prison where he found religion and structure. After becoming a minister and completing a ten-year sentence he found a job, got married, and became a pastor. Several years later he received another prison sentence. After two failed marriages, Alex still mistakenly believed that his problem was sin. His problem was low impulse control, and low resistance to sin was a result. He also had some deep wounds he received while living in the rural south where sharecropping was the major means of employment for Black Americans. Failure to address the underlying causes kept him in contention with sin.

During my childhood, my older brother pestered me for sport which became a major source of irritation. I couldn't successfully beat him up, so I said things that upset him. I loved the power words held and sought to hone that skill. He had a low tolerance for being ignored, so I added it to my arsenal and developed some bad habits that would later hinder my relationship with other people. As a teen I found masking my feelings and keeping my thoughts to myself the best way to handle challenges. By the time I was thirty years old I had learned I didn't need to defend myself—rebellion wasn't necessary—and I abandoned passive-aggressive behavior. I realized I was free to live the life I wanted and be who I wanted to be. I will talk more about this in the chapter on increasing our EI.

Avoiding emotional triggers can sometimes mean realizing when you can't help. Several years ago, a friend of mine was battling cancer. Not yet having any pastoral skills, I didn't know what else to do than be present. It was days before the holiday when I went by her home for a visit. She lamented she did not have the energy nor the time to prepare for the holiday in the way to which her family was accustomed. After I asked her how I could help, she ran off a long list of things that were impossible to do for her. The list was overwhelming. I later realized that I should have asked her to choose one thing from the list, but at the time I was paralyzed by her need. I realized later she didn't really want my help, instead wanting the ability and energy to do those things herself. Presence, in that instance, was probably the most appropriate thing to provide.

We creators are sensitive about our creations, and criticism can trigger ill feelings. In the book *The Heart of the Artist*, the author explains that creators are sensitive because God designed us to be. It takes creativity to make something that speaks God's will, prophesies or shows hidden beauty. It takes imagination to be creative, and there is a certain sensitivity that accompanies those gifts. When someone criticizes a creator, whether the creator is an artist, author, or preacher, it can cut to the core due the hard-wiring God felt necessary for the creator to possess.[3]

3. Nolan, *Heart of the Artist*, 10.

To raise your EI you will need to be honest with yourself. You may not be great at your current job because it involves dealing with your triggers all day every day. I had a job that required us to concentrate on making money while upper management insisted we focus on the organization's mission. Management held out the carrot in the form of hefty bonuses and expected us to pursue them. The organization's bottom line was to bring in the money, not advance the organization's mission as management claimed.

I remember being emotionally challenged on a job because my core values poorly matched with the company's mission. Though I liked my job assignment of managing other reps, I didn't like the changing culture. Initially I fully embraced the company's mission, but the mission was lost in the founder's desire to dominate the industry. There was a cult-like workplace environment due to the founder's demand for unquestioned loyalty. His intentions were great initially, but he eventually railed off into trying to destroy competitors. The founder groomed us to reject anything and anyone who did not buy into the company philosophy. A lot of good relationships with people in the lives of the employees were ruined.

If core values reflect our priorities, then the founder's priorities were matching the founder's new mission rather than the values that attracted us to the company. His motto had been "put God first, then family, and the company third." Yet his insistence that we distance ourselves from people who did not buy into the company's mission meant distancing ourselves from family members and friends. Family was important to me, and I could feel being pulled away from what made life happy. Trips to the office were depressing, and my bad mood led me to make some bad decisions. I found another job and eventually felt good about work and life in general.

Though the Holy Spirit is the "change agent," it is possible to hold the Holy Spirit at bay with thoughts and behavior that are contrary to God's desire for us. The Holy Spirit is always ready, though we may not be ready to give in to him at every turn. Instead of thinking of it as giving in, it might help to think of our engagement with the spirit as a partnership and partner's need to move in tandem with one another in order to achieve success. The more we feel commanded to do, the more likely we are to rebel, even though we signed up to be transformed to Christlikeness when we accepted Christ as our way to God.

During my younger years, the person with the lowest impulse control in any place or situation was likely to rob me of my peace. I once heard a security expert say that the best way to avoid a robbery is to prevent the opportunity. Rather than see myself as a victim I decided to research the underlying causes for low impulse control. Some of my frustration turned to empathy since autism is often characterized by low concentration, low impulse control, and bullying often caused by low self-esteem. Understanding that bullies are often victims of bullying by someone else gave me a new perspective.

Cognitive reframing helps too. It involves reimagining a scenario or outcome to a situation. For example, instead of thinking negative thoughts about why something is occurring, think positive thoughts about the opportunity it presents.

Our response to fruit development should be as purposeful and active as the Holy Spirit within us. Enhance the work of the Spirit by increasing your EI. If our minds consistently entertain biblical truths that support the best fruit production, we have an easier time staying free of self-defeating thoughts. The work of the spirit, your own core values, and your willingness to invest in your own spiritual growth will set you up for a successful way of living and thinking.

HERE ARE SOME SUGGESTIONS FOR HANDLING TRIGGERS

Recognize when you are anxious. Are your hands clasped tightly, sweating, high heart rate, sleepless, stomach in a knot, short tempered, or just plain scared? Control your breathing.

Wounds and trauma are not demons. They are underlying causes. Seek to get to the heart of what triggers you while managing the symptoms. Deep wounds take time to heal. If you have been praying for a miracle it may be that you are asking to skip the revelation, the discovery that leads to naming the real demons.

Ask yourself what causes you to think hopeless thoughts. For me it is not having enough help when I need it. Apostle Paul wrote, "Think on these things," meaning we concentrate on positive thoughts. "From the perspective of emotional intelligence, having hope means that one will not give in to overwhelming anxiety, a defeatist attitude, or depression in the face of challenges or setbacks. Indeed, people who are hopeful evidence less depression than others as they maneuver through life in pursuit of their goals, are less anxious in general, and have fewer emotional distresses."[4] Fortunately I have learned to recognize that when I have hopeless thoughts, I have likely underestimated how much time and energy a project would take to complete.

Loneliness can trigger depression. I had a psychologist tell me he recommended, to one of his patients suffering from depression, to eat before he arrived home since he lived alone and did not know how to cook. Eating out not only kept him in the company of other people and improved his mood, but meal prep was one less thing to worry about after he arrived home. A friend of mine lived alone too. I advised her to start putting on her crock pot before she left home and set a timer on the thermostat to turn on the heat in her house about 30 minutes before she planned to arrive home. That way her home would be warm when she arrived, and the smell of food would greet her. Being alone and loneliness are not the same thing. Though going home to an empty house can trigger a mood, introverts like me like being alone and shouldn't succumb to pressure to change our marital status.

Examine values and traditions you may have learned, but don't apply to your life or current thinking. Don't let guilt keep you bound to them, and put guilt in its place. Guilt is not what God is using to control you. God invites us to discover his love rather than drag us into remorse. Guilt is an emotion that is useful to recognize when we have done something wrong or need to do something right. It should not be what drives our lives. Guilt

4. Goleman, *Emotional Intelligence*, 78.

should not be something that inhibits your mental and spiritual growth or keeps you bound to traditions that don't work for you.

Dreams are very revealing and provide useful information about your mental state. It has been my observation that most dreams are not prophetic. Most dreams are not God speaking to you about the future. There are several things that affect one's dreams. Diet, poor health, watching television and social media just prior to sleeping, lack of exercise, mental illness, conversation with other people before bedtime, undigested food, alcohol, and drugs, to name a few. Yet dreams reveal what's literally on your mind. After my brother's sudden death I sought the help of a therapist. One of the practices she required me to adopt was writing down my dreams, since I was having nightmares. This was particularly distressing since I tend to have vivid dreams in full color. She explained to me that dreams are a window to the mind and can provide answers to emotional problems. She taught me how to understand my own thoughts and the effect trauma was having on my mental health and ability to sleep.

Another example: some years ago, I sat down at a table in my home and started sorting bills and writing checks to pay them. After a short while I lamented that my income was not enough to cover all my expenses. The ordeal put me in a bad mood. That same night I had a dream about two women. One was stout and short and the other was tall and lean. They both were wearing white clothing and looked very "religious" in their appearance. They both came into my home through an open door to the front of my house. While in my house they caused havoc and taunted me. After I awakened, I wrote down details of the dream as had been my custom. I interpreted the dream to mean that anxiety, represented by the stout person, and lack, presented as the lean person were able to gain access to my thinking because faith went out the window when I started trying to pay the bills. Frustration had flung the door wide open for anxiety to walk right in.

Drug and alcohol use ruins relationships because they alter mood. They affect the brain which is the center of emotional activity. You may not be an alcoholic but instead like the effect of substances. Given enough drugs or alcohol one may become impaired, and once impaired, your safety is at risk. I'm not against drinking but am against anything that puts you beyond your ability to make good decisions. There are people in my family who become not so nice when they drink, and a few become downright mean. It is all about mood and what affected their mood. For them alcohol is a trigger that needs to be avoided not just for their sake but for the sake of their relationship with the rest of our family.

Triggers can sometimes be other people. There was a certain family member I used to avoid because I didn't like his conversation. I asked myself what exactly I didn't like about him, then realized there was something about the past I had not reconciled. It wasn't as much about his conversation as it was about past hurts. Initially I decided I just wasn't going to care anymore and found not caring an effective short-term solution to mood management. After a few years I decided to confront him, knowing that the conversation might not result in any apology or change. The person didn't apologize but instead blamed me for his abusive behavior. In addition to just getting that off my chest I had peace knowing he knew my feelings concerning how he treated me, and I started making my way to forgiveness.

Having sensitive subjects people avoid discussing with you is a clear indication you have unresolved issues. What are subjects people don't want to raise with you? Some may be due to trauma. Trauma is not always caused by something cataclysmic. Abandonment issues from being left behind during childhood can haunt you well into adulthood. A parent leaving the family, temporary separations, or a parent being emotionally unavailable can lead to abandonment issues. When I was a young child, my mom went to the hospital for several days. That event caused a reoccurring nightmare that haunted me until I realized I had been traumatized by my mother's absence.

It is beneficial to note why something changes your mood and address why it triggers negative thoughts. Nothing changes my dad's mood faster than a money issue. My dad is old school and born during the great depression. He doesn't like to throw anything away that he feels is still useful or spend money unnecessarily. To be honest I'm the same way. Rearing kids changed that for me. Their needs and emergencies weren't based on my mood but on life in general. I've grown to be much more accepting of challenges that need financing. Are you the same way?

Health issues can trigger bad moods. In this country obesity is a problem. Diet and exercise can help even if you are not overweight. Exercise helps your mood by increasing endorphins. "What are endorphins? Endorphins are chemicals (hormones) your body releases when it feels pain or stress. They're released during pleasurable activities such as exercise, massage, eating and sex too. Endorphins help relieve pain, reduce stress and improve your sense of well-being."[5] Exercise doesn't have to be boring or stressful. Walks, biking, tai chi, swimming, and other exercises that raise your heart rate help with mood management.

Food can affect your mood, and sugar and caffeine are mood changers. Just ask anyone who loves dessert. A good mood is desirable, but the crash after the sugar intake isn't. Deficiencies are mood changers too, and food allergies are a struggle for some of us. After multiple trips to the allergist and several endoscopies, I was able to identify food allergies and ways to manage them.

Stress is a mood changer. Jobs, childcare, health issues, coworkers, difficult people, deadlines of any kind, changing locations, unrealistic expectations, to name a few. Fad diets can cause stress. My coworkers and I went on a rotation diet together. There were days we were required to eat no more than 600, 900, and 1200 calories. After the first week we were in a bad mood, were short with each other, and found it hard to concentrate on our work. We all worked in the same office, which made it even more challenging to get along. We realized what was happening but decided that we would support each other and finish what we started. We laughed later about what our family members said about our behavior and the lack of seasoning in meals we cooked for them during those three weeks.

Unrealistic expectations are stress producing. Examine why you take on too much. My mother had high expectations of her

5. "Endorphins."

children, and as a result, I became an overachiever. In recent years I have learned to dial back my self-expectations, avoid taking on too many tasks, and concentrate on what gives me the greatest joy and self-satisfaction. I've learned the hard way that the older we become, the longer it takes to recover from being exhausted. Assess how much energy you have and stop short of using all of it. Exhaustion can make you negative, grouchy, susceptible to illnesses, and otherwise hard to get along with. If you are always tired see your physician.

Being responsible for other people's finances can cause stress. As a pastor and a development officer I assisted people with their estate plans and assisted people who handled the estates of others. Give a lot of thought to accepting responsibility for handling estates and inheritances. Being a power of attorney or executer of an estate means being responsible for making decisions that affect the lives of other people who may not appreciate the decisions you make, and some decisions may be harder than you anticipated. Get some advice prior to taking on that role.

Pets can be comforting, yet some can be expensive or destructive. Difficult pet behavior can be the opposite of emotional support. It can be heartbreaking to give up a pet, but your emotional health is important. Consider a reputable shelter if you cannot locate someone to adopt your pet if you are unable to secure a trainer. A friend gave me a kitten when I lived alone. He thought it would be a good idea for me to have a feral kitten he found on the street. In just a week that kitten had destroyed my drapes, done his business in my planters, and torn up part of my couch, not to mention he had fleas. As much as I appreciated my friend wanting me to have a pet, I recognized the pet he gave me wasn't one that fit my lifestyle or temperament. I found the kitten a good home.

Insufficient sunlight affects some people. Natural sunlight is particularly important to people of color.[6] Vitamin D is a crucial element in being and staying mentally and physically healthy. If you can't get outdoors, a sunlamp and/or vitamin D supplement may work.

6. Salomon, "Does Vitamin D Deficiency."

Goodness and/or spiritual energy is often referred to as light, and Paul refers to it in his letters. Fruit trees and bushes get their power from the sun, and it is important that plants are situated in places where the sun is not blocked. In addition to getting some sun, situate yourself in places where the light of Christ is present. A prayer or support group, a place of worship or an actual community garden would be good places to find positive spiritual energy.

The spirit of God you possess may be far more ready to cultivate some change than you are willing to accommodate. It happens. Part of cultivation is reproof, and reproof doesn't feel very good. Yet if we are to imitate God then what is most not like God must go. Be honest about not being ready to let some things or habits go. That is part of maturity too.

Loss of control and sudden transitions can be triggering for some people. My grandson is a lovable, fun, intelligent kid, yet when it is time to change from one activity to another his mood changes, and he doesn't transition well. A sudden change in plans throws him off emotionally. You may also be hardwired this way. A life coach can help you adopt practices that work for you.

Racism is a trigger. Some find it difficult to attain emotional security while experiencing the challenges racism presents. Change is slow, and racism will always exist, yet we can control our response to it. High emotional and spiritual maturity lead to the best response to challenges that are intentionally imposed.

Overstimulation can trigger emotions. After I cook an elaborate meal or meal for invited guest, I'm no longer hungry. Trying an involved new recipe or cooking for company is stressful for me. After I accomplish that feat, I'm overstimulated and no longer in the best mood. Author Robyn Samuels suggests that after cooking a meal you may not want it due to overstimulation. She offers a theory and suggestion: "Because your olfactory system is in overdrive and overstimulated, the most obvious solution would be to cook quicker meals. In the same way that some people forget to eat when preoccupied, working or spending more time in the kitchen may result a decreased appetite. . . Preparing quicker meals could result in an improved appetite after cooking."[7]

Rejection is a trigger too. I realize while writing this book, someone will eventually challenge my beliefs, and my book will not be accepted in some arenas. Rather than rail off emotionally I can prepare to accept those facts, be confident about my accomplishments, and practice self-control as ways of managing my emotions. Also, walking in the spirit is my path to peace, and the peace I obtain does not depend on what other people accept.

A change in marital status presents a variety of issues. Some years ago, I was newly separated, and instead of living in a new, spacious house with an attached garage with my husband I was now living on the second floor of an apartment building. Every time I had to bring in the groceries from the car by myself, I complained about my circumstances and swore that if I had a good husband, I wouldn't have to do this. When the weather was bad, I felt even worse. Once the groceries were put away and I relaxed, I was fine appreciating my life and family for what they were. This scenario went on for a while, since failing to realize the challenge of bringing in the bags without help kept me in the negative emotional loop.

Having to wait can trigger impatience. Some doors to opportunities you will have to wait for God to open. Patience is a fruit of the Spirit that can take a lifetime to develop, but it tends to increase with age. While waiting for opportunities, tend to the character the Holy Spirit is cultivating. Practicing patience isn't easy but is necessary for high EI.

Indulge in what is comforting and changes your mood: a hot shower or bubble bath, a long walk, a new haircut or style. My mother used to find rearranging our living room helped her mood. I find a new hair style to be a mood booster. Videos and movies that are inspirational also help, as does practicing gratitude. *Emotional Intelligence 2.0* by Travis Bradberry is an excellent resource with multiple suggestions on how to manage your mood.

7. Samuels, "Why Don't I Have an Appetite."

Book and articles on positive psychology hold knowledge about EI. Wicks offers, "Positive psychology is not a psychological 'concealer' that hides the real blemishes of life, nor is it an emotional or spiritual cortisone that temporarily eliminates unpleasant life experiences. Instead, it is a more dynamic way for people to view their state of being and be freed from the bindings of a solely negative focus. Although positive psychology is centered upon the individual, it also integrates the strengths of supporting institutions such as families, schools, and churches, so it is a natural approach for persons involved in pastoral ministry."[8]

Hopefully the Christian leader with high emotional intelligence recognizes the need for rest. Part of self-awareness is recognizing when you're too often doing someone else's work or projects that can be best completed by another person. You may have unrealistic self-expectations about bringing an idea to fruition, or perhaps you are a bit of a perfectionist, not wanting anyone to help you. You may be overriding the Holy Spirit to meet goals. You may be experiencing mental as well as physical fatigue due to your unwillingness to turn things over to someone else.

Review your triggers to see if you are making progress. Keep a journal. Walk like you have confidence until you have it. Throw your shoulders back, and keep your head up. Decide who you want to be rather than what others want you to be. I once dated a guy who was happiest when I was not nice to him. He often aggravated me until I became mean and irritated. I'm not sure why he loved my negative response so much. I decided that was not who I wanted to be, so I dumped him and endeavored to be a better person.

8. Wicks and Bucks, Reframing for Change, 9

8

How to Increase Your EI and Resources

Appeal to your higher power and be open to change. We Christians are not without power. We were promised the helper, and we have him. Paul speaks in his letter to Christians at Philippi with the level of spiritual and emotional maturity he has obtained. He explains that he is capable of living in whatever circumstance befalls him, whether good or bad, plentiful or meager. He goes on to say that "... I have learned the secret of being filled and going hungry, both of having abundance and suffering need. I can do all things through Him who strengthens me" (Phil 4:12–13). Paul recognizes he has a source of strength to draw on during any circumstance.

Practicing spiritual discipline helps you grow emotionally as well as spiritually. Some of the same practices that therapists recommend dealing with emotional issues are listed as spiritual discipline in Richard Foster's book *Celebration of Discipline: The Path to Spiritual Growth*. Prayer, meditation, journaling, fasting, and study are a few of the disciplines explained in his book. Foster writes that willpower is not enough to break ingrained bad habits. He writes "the disciplines" are necessary for godly transformation.

Foster also wrote *Prayer: Finding the Heart's True Home*. Foster describes different kinds of prayer and how they originate. I highly recommend prayer to improve your emotional health.

Don't beat yourself up if all your prayers sound the same. Prayers reflect where we are emotionally. Prayer allows you to hear yourself and unburden yourself from things that are beyond your control. Prayer is talking to God, and unlike talking with people, God has no boundaries or subjects that he finds to sensitive to discuss.

Some people would find it sacrilegious to write down prayers before you pray them. Reading what you write is another way to hear yourself. After you write some prayers, ask yourself if all your prayers sound the same. Are they a list of nonstop requests? Analyze them and look for love, sacrifice, and service. Are those three things absent? If there is something happening in your life that has you feeling overwhelmed, then service may not be something you are able to wrap your head around. Don't worry about it. Trust God to get you through what is happening unless he is showing you that service is key to your transitioning in and through your situation.

Foster wrote, "Celebration brings joy into life and joy makes us strong. Scripture tells us that the joy of the Lord is our strength (Neh 8:10). We cannot continue long in anything without it." Foster attests that anything we endeavor to do that is challenging we will continue to do if joy is eminent. He goes on to say that "God brings about the transformation of our lives through the Disciplines, and we will not know genuine joy until there is a transforming work within us."[1] Foster suggests singing, dancing and shouting as ways to practice celebration. Other ways he suggests are family events, life changes, and cultural festivals.

New skills need to be practiced, tested for improvement and to gain feedback. God did not create you to be alone anyway, so avoid constant isolation. I had a close friend who was homebound due to health issues, and he taught himself scripture daily. Initially he was open to discussion and didn't mind having his theology tested. After a few years he became less open to challenge and instead saw himself as an authority on Scripture. Our last conversation didn't go well. I called to see how he was doing, and he only wanted to discuss his latest epiphany. After trying to change the subject a few times, I realized that he wasn't open to discussion but

1. Foster, *Celebration of Discipline*, 193.

only to forcing his interpretation of Scripture. He became increasingly agitated, so I ended the call.

Which brings us to reading the Bible. The Bible is a guide to life and holds encouragement and inspiration for every situation. The Bible holds information about who God is, his moods, and how God moves. Don't start reading just anywhere; start with an online directed study or ask a trusted friend or a pastor to help you. If you can afford a study Bible or study Bible app, purchase one. Paul is not the only author who wrote about adapting behaviors that lead to spiritual growth and wholeness.

Reading a Bible unassisted can be confusing and frustrating. Some parts of the Bible appear to contradict other parts. A directed study or course related to biblical truths or subjects of interest to you will help your understanding. Please note that the Bible was written during ancient times, and some words and symbols should be studied in context with the time they were written. Read first for encouragement and wisdom. As you gain understanding, read for enlightenment and growth.

You don't have to be Christian to gain wisdom and knowledge from reading a Bible. The book of Proverbs (proverbial wisdom) is easy to understand, especially if you use an amplified or modern translation version. Memorize the list of the fruit of the spirit. Paul often spoke and wrote about "the mind," meaning that the way to and pursuit of right standing included engaging your thinking along with your spirit. Paul preached holistic improvement that includes the mind, body, and spirit. Reading is one way to engage your mind and spirit, and the Bible is full of people whose lives and issues parallel ours. Reading about them and their walk will allow you to learn from their successes and mistakes as well as gain motivation and understanding related to your challenges.

Making an effort to walk in the Spirit will also include engaging in something that changes your mood or praying for help to get out of the mood. Consistently recognizing when your mood needs changing is self-awareness and a sign of real growth. Remind yourself that the Spirit is at work and avoid using the unfinished work as an excuse to continue whatever habits you haven't yet mastered.

Mood is only part of the transition. Transition requires faith and you must believe you have the power to grow and change. Believe that you will experience God in new and exciting ways. Walking in the Spirit is aligning your thoughts with God's and adapting behavior that exhibits good Christian virtues. It is the Spirit of God within you that is guiding your transformation and anticipate that you will draw nearer to him while he is doing so.

Perspective and discernment mean a lot when dealing with others. When the church is at its best, the love of Jesus is demonstrated. When people have issues, their issues sometimes manifest in unhealthy ways that hurt other people. The church consists of people, so when people speak of church hurt, they are referring to being hurt by people in the church. It happens. I pastored a church that was transitioning to closing. There was a lot of pain and unhappiness associated with the church and its circumstances, which is why some members had already left before I assumed the helm. I refused to take personally things members said out of anger and disappointment because I realized their anger was misplaced.

Practicing what promotes high emotional intelligence is how I stayed above negative comments and passive aggressive behavior members displayed. Rather than retaliate, I focused on the goal while having compassion, did a lot of listening and discerning what members really needed, and chose to love, even when it didn't seem to make a difference. Eventually the church closed but not before I had formed some good relationships with people that lasted for years. Also, my own confession and repentance augmented the work of the Spirit. In these situations, choose love, choose to be discerning, practice kindness, and seek opportunities for bonding and promoting understanding. Church is a good place to practice what increases your EI and fruit production.

As a pastor I often prayed for people and their problems. It was interesting what people requested I pray for. They often asked for mitigation from the problems and relief from the symptoms, i.e. body pain, stress at work or home, not enough money, self-esteem and relationship issues. Symptoms are not underlying causes. Pain and fear are symptoms not an underlying cause. Pain and fear originate from somewhere. Medical experts often treat symptoms without adequately explaining causes. There is a difference between urgent care and seeing a specialist. Healers with miracle gifts can treat your symptoms, which can grant you presence of mind and temporary freedom. Yet problems manifest some other way because the underlying cause has not been addressed. Often people stop taking their meds because they feel better. Yet they are not cured because the underlying cause of their condition or infection has not been fully eradicated.

Faith and hope promote positivity, so practice staying optimistic as much as possible. That does not mean you aren't realistic about life. I once had a "glass half-empty" way of seeing life but decided to change that. It took some practice, and it still does. Putting a limit on the amount of bad news you take in daily helps with maintaining a positive outlook. Some occupations, like mine, require listening to other people's issues. When I worked my seasonal job as a catastrophe claims processor in the escalation department, customers didn't reach me unless they had problems that weren't resolved by someone else. When I wasn't working, I found something else to do besides taking in more bad news.

Our society offers a lot of emotional junk food. An athlete who aspires to obtain the best possible performance doesn't feed themselves junk. The person aspiring to increase their emotional intelligence shouldn't feed themselves emotional junk food but feed themselves whatever supports emotional intelligence and good emotional health. Television, social media, books, and music not only affect your mood but can put tension in our experience as believers. When we experience cognitive dissonance, we should ask ourselves if what we are daily subjecting ourselves to improves or stalls our attempts at raising our EI to augment our engagement with the spirit of God.

Spiritual mentors can assist with our attempt to raise our EI through self-awareness. Wicks offers, "To accomplish this depth of self-awareness so that change becomes more readily possible, several steps can be either taken by oneself or with a spiritual director, formator or counselor. They include exploring the cognitive appraisal of an event, revisiting the emotional arousal it caused, and examining the resulting behavior that one undertook. As part of this recollecting process, it is important that both the objective (what actually happened) and the subjective (what beliefs and judgments one has made about the event) be examined."[2]

Make a list of things in your life that are stress producing. Attempt to find patterns or common denominators. Stress affects not only your peace but your ability to get along with other people. For example, does your insistence on buying things brand new instead of used cause you to overspend or feel upset when you can't afford what you want? Does the mood spread to your significant other? Ask yourself why a used item is not acceptable. Think about what is necessary to buy new and when used items are your best option according to your budget. Also think about whether going over budget to get someone new will put you in contention with your loved ones.

Writing my story about my own past helped me to understand why I formed habits, made certain decisions, and discovered my purpose. Asking some relatives to help me remember events that I had forgotten and their filling in missing pieces offered other perspectives with which I could use to analyze my past. Their comments were also helpful in helping me see how they saw me in past events. I had a conversation with my older cousin who helped me to understand traumatic events in my mom's past. My cousin said she often thought of me and sympathized with how much burden I had to carry. I was surprised because I didn't realize any extended family members were paying attention.

Self-awareness includes discerning when a person wants you to change so they don't have to. Coaching can help us see ourselves the way others see us. A coach that specializes in spiritual or leadership development can help you with increasing your IE and fruit development. Do your homework and choose someone that is not only relatable but has a great track record for success. Not everyone who claims to be a coach is gifted. Some people are great cheerleaders while others are great coaches. The difference between

2. Wicks and Bucks, *Reframing for Change*, 10.

the two is a cheerleader often stops cheering when the team is losing, and the coach stays until the end of the game and longer. A coach knows how to get the best from the player and recognizes the player's strengths, weaknesses, family situation, and how the player thinks of him or herself. Choose someone who will make an investment in your success and take personally your desire to improve.

Counseling and therapy are not the same as coaching. Raising your EI may require you to unpack some trauma or other psychological issues. Everyone should commit to counseling at least a few times in life. It is worth it. You may need someone to help you identify the causes of bad habits, negative thinking, and whatever produces stress.

Wicks says this about counseling: "However at this juncture, ministry needs to incorporate not just past understandings of the human condition, but also must seek to employ other more recent advances in psychology to foster the pastoral care functions of healing, nurturing, guiding, reconciling and change. This can be done by employing the findings and publications on both cognitive-behavioral therapy and positive psychology."[3] I'm not advocating for positive psychology methods, though I agree with Wick in that positive action follows positive thoughts. Paul's premise in 2 Corinthians is that thinking on "these things" leads to positive behavior and righteousness.

I am not recommending any specific psychological therapy. I am, though, a proponent of therapy intended to assist people with developing a mindset that helps them experience God more fully and love themselves and their neighbor wholeheartedly. During recovery from traumatic events, don't skip counseling, doctors appointments, and group activities. Change is in process even after the dramatic or traumatic event is over. Tend to your healing, recovery, or restoration. Some patients stop taking medicine when they feel better when the doctor's instructions clearly state "finish all the medication." I'm advising the same for your spiritual and mental growth. Don't stop halfway just because you see some improvement. Keep going and bearing good fruit your entire life.

3. Wicks and Bucks, *Reframing for Change*, 10.

Trauma may cause you to evaluate your religious beliefs. When my brother died by suicide, in an attempt to understand his actions, I chose to reevaluate my beliefs. I later learned it is common to do just that while grieving. It may not take something so traumatic for you to evaluate what you believe and why you believe it. God is with you even in your evaluation and can welcome your questions.

Take note of your own cultural values. Is your quest to have more, get married, have children, attain a certain status, join the family business, or partake of religious rituals causing you stress? Do you fail to address conflict due to family hierarchies, traditions, or social norms? A study by Gunkel, Schlaegel, and Taras shows the relationship between conflict resolution styles and cultural values: "The results of structural equations modeling and mediation analysis show that in particular uncertainty avoidance and long-term orientation influence preferences for the conflict handling styles of compromising, obliging, and integrating through emotional intelligence. Furthermore, we find that collectivism has a direct negative effect on the preference for a dominating style and that power distance has a direct positive effect on the preference for an avoiding and dominating style."[4] Power distance is the distance between the highest and lowest person on the hierarchy.

How do we address conflict with family, coworkers, partners, and friends in an emotionally mature way that reflects our Christian and/cultural values? I attended a workshop held by a ministerial colleague who was also marketing her services. She said at the beginning of the workshop, "I'm nice as long as you are nice." I don't remember reading where Jesus or Paul said that. Her need to make that remark made me uneasy since perception matters and misunderstanding eventually happen in any relationship and had to consider whether her of way of heading of conflict would work for me. Although she seemed competent professionally, I chose not to use her services. Consider your conflict resolution style and whether it best suits the clientele you desire to attract.

Low EI can be the result of conditioning. Some parents of baby boomers said things to their kids like "fix your face, stop

4. Gunkel et al., *Cultural Values*, 568.

crying or I'll give you something to cry about" and "don't tell anyone what goes on in this house." We grew up either turning inward or learning how to hide our emotions. Since we of the next generation of children learned to be self-reliant, independent, and civil, parents believed that style of parenting worked. Anxiety, frustration, and depression develop in children that aren't allowed to express themselves.

By the time I was a young adult I had developed some bad habits and took living life on my own terms to an extreme. It made it hard for me to develop lasting relationships. I lacked compassion, patience with other people's shortcomings and empathy, often choosing to ignore people who disappointed me. Over the years I had to deprogram myself, and it took a long time. Yet I decided who I wanted to be and chose not to engage with people who couldn't appreciate me and the fruit the Holy Spirit was producing. I found counseling, books, and other resources dedicated to understanding suppressed emotions to be good resources of information. An old book I read as a teen called *The Power of Positive Thinking* helped me considerably.

It is very important to your mental and spiritual growth for you to own your complicated past and forgive yourself while you endeavor to be better. Forgiveness is a process, and it is imperative for you to make your way to forgiveness as you walk in the spirit. If it was possible to erase your past, you would probably erase the very experiences God will use to bring about change or encouragement to someone else's life or to the world in general.

To increase my social awareness, I endeavored to be a better listener. Pastors are accustomed to preaching and are the ones who do the talking. Yet good pastoral care involves listening. You can discover things about yourself by listening to others. Also, instead of retreating from problems in my relationships, I asked what it is that makes a particular issue problematic. As a teenager I discovered people who I believed to be my friends were people who just wanted to ride in my new car.

Travis Bradberry offers social awareness strategies. One strategy he suggests is to plan for social gatherings. "The next time you RSVP for an event, in your next breath remind yourself to plan. On an index card list who is going to be at the event and list any talking points or do's. Don't be shy; carry the list with you."[5] When I was in my early twenties, I would listen to sports radio in my car on the way to parties so that I would have something to talk about with guys after I arrived. I realized that I only needed to start the conversation and sports enthusiasts would carry the rest of the conversation.

Bradberry also offers, "Catch the mood in the room. Here is how you can catch the mood in the room. When you enter the room, scan it and notice whether you feel and see energy or quiet, subdued calm. Take notice of how people are arranging themselves—alone or in group."[6] This is something that was hard for me to master. I'm not comfortable breaking into a group, but I take a chance to observe how the conversation is going. I may step away to return a phone to excuse myself from groups that aren't welcoming.

Be intentional when honing your communication skills. Listen to your own tone when you speak with other people, especially during a disagreement. I'm always surprised how effectively controlling my breathing helps me feel less tense. After controlling my breathing for a few minutes, my whole body relaxes.

When assuming the helm at a new company or organization, people will leave. It isn't personal; it always happens. There will be people who stay who don't take change well, and here is where high emotional intelligence is important. It isn't that they are bad people or intentionally trying to be difficult. Have a plan for how to make the transition as easy as possible even when or if you need to let people go. If you have experience in transitional leadership that's great. If not consult some resources that have proven effective where trust is an issue.

Leading isn't easy, but leading with EI certainly has the potential to be more fulfilling. High social awareness means that we are able to make decisions based on empathy and understanding as well as access the strengths and weakness of other people. It is

5. Bradberry, *Emotional Intelligence 2.0*, 151.

6. Bradberry, *Emotional Intelligence 2.0*, 174.

harder to trust someone who is led by their emotions since logic and the ability to rationalize is diminished. King Saul in the book of 1 Samuel was a leader who suffered from jealousy and poor emotional health. Music changed his mood but not his emotional quotient. When he knew he'd made poor choices, repentance and resolutions were made but were short-lived. Saul compromised instructions given to him and instead acted on impulses which put others in jeopardy. Jealousy and paranoia derailed him, and he was prone to violence, even throwing a spear at someone during dinner. He died a violent death by his own hands. Bad things can happen when leaders don't manage their emotions well. Low emotion intelligence leaves us struggling with our mood and the effects of poor decision making.

Great leaders avoid taking insults personally. That doesn't mean they put up with abuse. It does mean people will not be able to control their mood or what they think of themselves. They realize not everyone who reports to them will like them. Leaders with high EI practice self-acceptance. Appreciate who you are and the best version of yourself you are attempting to become yet be approachable and your request obtainable. Ask a person who constantly complains to remedy the situation. Request they solve the problem, something I learned from parenting my kids.

When you are leading be prepared to be misunderstood. When I find myself in a chaotic situation the leader in me rises to the occasion. My emotional intelligence allows me to maintain mental stability while I analyze, lead, and/or assist. People who don't know me well sometimes get the impression I lack empathy due to my facial expressions and my asking poignant questions. I sometimes come off as being cold, but that is not who I am. No, it is instead the Holy Spirit in me helping me run on all cylinders to create appropriate responses and/or remedies.

My dad asked me, after reading my first book on transitional ministry, how I kept from becoming angry or bitter with people who constantly got in the way of my trying to help. I explained that it was essential for me to remind myself who I really worked for and why I was trying to help. Otherwise, I explained, it would have been easy to become resentful and bitter, especially when I was not financially compensated by people needing assistance. I remind myself of what apostle Paul said when he advocated for Onesimus in the book of Philemon: "If then you regard me *as* a partner, accept him as *you would* me. But if he has wronged you in any way or owes *you anything*, charge that to my account" (Phlm 1:17–18). I accepted that I was in partnership with God and charged what I felt I was due to his account.

Mothers are leaders too, and children teach us a lot about social awareness. My kids have caused me to take more time to think before I respond unless a situation requires immediate action. Children will hang onto every word especially when they are trying to be persuasive. The right answer may not be the most appropriate one. One of my mentors spoke slowly as if his life depended on his word choices. I initially believed it was cultural until I became a pastor and discovered that people can ask really hard questions impromptu, and to take my time answering.

As Christians we should model a life of service. Foster writes "The service disciplines the feelings rather than allowing the feeling to control the service."[7] True service is given when there is a need. True service is born out of altruism. Foster also explains that "Of all the classical Spiritual Disciplines, service is the most conductive to the growth of humility."[8] Researching religious beliefs or asking a person about their faith shows you are interested in them, which can help with your understanding as a service provider.

Access your life. Is it lined up with what Paul describes as Christian virtues? Could you be better at displaying any of the virtues that Paul lists? How are your relationships with other people? Are there people you avoid because the outcome of your engagement with them is not what you desire? Have you lost and/or left multiple jobs in a short period of time? Is it you or the choices you make that lead to either discontent, confusion, or bad feelings toward coworkers and bosses? I've seen more people consistently lose jobs due to low EI more than for any other reason. Do an

7. Foster, *Celebration of Discipline*, 130.

8. Foster, *Celebration of Discipline*, 130.

honest self-assessment of your life and engagement with other people so that you can see where improvement is needed.

RESOURCES

VIA Institute has resources to help you with self-discovery and change. Take the VIA survey or another personality test to discover your strengths and weaknesses. When I applied for seminary, as well as when I took my first class on EI, I was required to ask people who knew me to answer questions about my personality. The survey answers were anonymously given, but a summary of the results was shared with me, which I took to heart. Try it. When I took the survey for emotional intelligence, I scored lowest in "reading the room" and sought to work on that. Why read the room? Before you launch into your agenda, it is a good idea to find out what other people are feeling. I didn't score low in this trait; I just scored lower on this one than on the others.

Bible colleges and seminaries offer spiritual formation classes, and you're never too old to go to school. There are schools and universities that offer certificate programs in emotional intelligence. Also, leadership training that includes EI as continuing education helps you remain current. EI certificates are added to your resume or CV. Workshops are offerings that require less of a time commitment than enrolling in school. Fortunately, Zoom has provided an alternative to in-person attendance.

"Finally, seminaries could support growth in emotional intelligence by structuring some of their courses as laboratories for learning rather than as academic presentations. Within a laboratory format, students would be encouraged to offer each other feedback on the impact their words and behavior have on each other. Most people are unlikely to change their behavior until they hear from others how those words and behaviors impact them in a negative way."[9]

9. Ott, *Emotional Intelligence*, 112.

Spiritual gifts inventories help you assess your own gifts, which can provide insight into how best to serve your place of worship and community accordingly. Check with your pastor to see if he or she recommends any survey or website.

Paul has given a list of virtues and explains that what runs contrary to good spiritual health may certainly squelch the work of the Spirit. Paul, the author of 1 Thess, explained, "Do not quench the Spirit; do not despise prophetic utterances. But examine everything carefully; hold fast to that which is good; abstain from every form of evil" (1 Thess 5:18–22). Paul explained in the prior verses to help the weak, practice gratitude, pray, rejoice, and do not return evil for evil. This is a description of high emotional intelligence.

"Emotional learning involves growing new pathways at the neurological level, not just adding more input to the existing (status quo). New ways of living, responding, and understanding oneself involve creating new circuits and replacing older, less adaptive ones."[10] Change takes time, and each of us will always have our foibles. Keep going and growing, persevering and leading. God told Cain, "You must master it. If you do well, will not *your countenance* be lifted up? And if you do not do well, sin is crouching at the door; and its desire is for you, but you must master it" (Gen 4:7). Sin "waits at the door," which means sin presents itself as opportunity when you are most vulnerable.

There will eventually come some situations in life that are more than you can handle by yourself. Why believe in God then not trust him with things that are beyond your control? The Holy Spirit is at work and will bring your transformation to completion. Spiritual mentors, experienced with spiritual formation, can help you discern what will bring you closer to God while you mature emotionally and spiritually. There are times when all you can do is trust, keep your composure, and wait. "Wait on the Lord and be of good courage, he will strengthen your heart" (Isa 40:31).

Finally, teach emotional management to your children in the context of Christian development and spiritual formation. "Using the Frog Street curriculum, teachers are taught to manage their

10. Steven Ott, "Emotional Intelligence," 20.

thoughts, feelings, and actions in the face of daily stressors, and to then teach these skills to children. The seven skills, or core components, include composure, assertiveness, encouragement, choices, empathy, positive intent, and consequences. Using structures, rituals, and routines, instead of scripted lessons presented at certain times each day, teachers look for teachable moments to share the seven skills with children."[11]

RECOMMENDED SCRIPTURE VERSES

Ephesians 4:22—". . . that, in reference to your former manner of life, you lay aside the old self, which is being corrupted in accordance with the lusts of deceit, and that you be renewed in the spirit of your mind, and put on the new self, which in the likeness of God has been created in righteousness and holiness of the truth."

First Corinthians 10:13—"No temptation has overtaken you that is not common to man. God is faithful, and he will not let you be tempted beyond your ability, but with the temptation he will also provide the way of escape, that you may be able to endure it."

Second Timothy 1:7—"For God gave us a spirit not of fear but of power and love and self-control."

Romans 12:2—"Do not be conformed to this world, but be transformed by the renewal of your mind, that by testing you may discern what is the will of God, what is good and acceptable and perfect."

Philippians 2:3–4—"Do nothing from selfish ambition or conceit, but in humility count others more significant than yourselves. Let each of you look not only to his own interests, but also to the interests of others."

11. Frady, "Spiritual Formation," 403.

In 1 Samuel 25, the story of Abigail reads like a modern movie. Abigail was wise and possessed high emotional intelligence, running toward the problem instead of away from it. She de-escalated the situation and brought about peace. Her actions saved lives.

RECOMMENDED READING

Celebration of Discipline by Richard Foster

Cultivating the Fruit of the Spirit by W. J. H. Wright

Emotional Intelligence by Daniel Goleman

Emotional Intelligence 2.0 by Travis Bradberry and Jean Greaves. It has an exhaustive list of steps to increase your EI. There is also a workbook.

The Heart of the Artist by Rory Noland

Primal Leadership by Daniel Goleman, Richard Boyatzis, and Annie McKee

Resonant Leadership by Richard Boyatzis and Annie McKee

Conclusion

"But the fruit of the Spirit is love, joy, peace, patience, kindness, goodness, faithfulness, gentleness, self-control; against such things there is no law" (Gal 5:22–23).

THE PURPOSE OF THIS book is not to convince you there is a God, nor is it to persuade anyone to commit to existential thinking. If you believe there is a God, and his Spirit is at work within you, you are already capable of existential thinking. The purpose of this book is to encourage hope and transformation in the believer. If you believe the Holy Spirit is at work, practice what will augment the work. Though the Holy Spirit is our change agent, our spiritual and emotional maturity determines our response to what the Spirit is doing.

Both Goleman and Paul believe character can be affected by what we practice. What we practice helps our temperament and ability to handle challenges, yet self-help alone does not transform the spirit. Paul addresses the condition of the human Spirit. Goleman addresses the workings of the mind and engagement of mind with emotion. I believe whatever methods we employ to improve our emotional intelligence and integrity need to be supported by biblical truths. I hope my attempt at extolling the value of high emotional intelligence with the support of biblical principles has been successful. I hope there is a ripple effect from reading this book that causes others to be better able to walk in the Spirit.

Spiritualists maintain that we experience life cycles. There are some situations that occur repeatedly during our lives. Some situations repeatedly occur due to our life choices, yet others occur due to God's purposes in our lives. Our response in those situations should mature more each time we encounter them if we purpose to raise our awareness, trust, and emotional capital.

There will be things in life that may cause us to become bitter. Being passed over, unloved, last in line, betrayed, or abandoned can lead to feelings of inadequacy, paranoia, or anger. The person with high emotional intelligence will determine what feelings to abandon to start the process of healing while rising above negative thoughts. The spiritual person with high emotional intelligence has the potential to discern what virtues to adopt for emotional and spiritual sustainability.

Hope, growth, and faith matter at every stage of life. Despite my challenges growing up I made no excuses and imagined myself a winner. My desire to make it in life, along with my being determined to rise above my circumstances regardless of how challenging, kept me going. My faith in God supported my determination, and I never lost hope. I somehow felt my challenges were temporary, believing my higher power was at work, and at times believed God was all I needed for protection and sustainability. That is not to say there were no low points, emotional scars, or need for therapy to keep moving in a positive direction. It means that faith, resilience, patience, and managing my emotions worked for me.

Decide who you want to be and consider how it will affect your brand. When I was a young girl, I settled my issues with other kids by fighting and throwing rocks. One day my friend Robin hit a boy in the head with a brick. I took him to my mom since his caregivers were not home. My mom did her best to tend to his injury. To this day the incident is attributed to me. I didn't hit the boy; my friend did. Yet that was my way of settling issues, so the allegations stuck.

Each of us is unique, and some people may not like you. Rather than letting others cause you to despise your position, ask God to show you his plans for your uniqueness and accept it and your role in the world. Embrace the changes God leads you through and the fruit he is cultivating. God is a loving, faithful, caring and thoughtful cultivator. We should endeavor to be like him when dealing with ourselves and other people.

Not everyone who experiences trauma can hear God or think their way to better emotional health without assistance. I hope this book helps a young person better understand how they arrived and they attempt to practice raising their EI while God handles their circumstances.

Paul gives instructions, in his dissertation, for Christian conduct and maintaining godly virtue. In the previous chapter Paul describes behavior that leads to trouble and problems. He describes what will cause a Christian to veer off into a fallen condition. Low emotional intelligence lends itself to making regrettable decisions. Paul emphasizes the freedom salvation affords us and with that freedom and love we should love and serve others. If a Christian is to live a life of freedom, he or she are advised to ascribe to the behavior that produces good fruit, showing their desire to live "by the Spirit."

Paul explains in the same paragraph on fruit that Christians are not without help. The Holy Spirit oversees cultivation, and the spiritually mature Christian responds by following the spirit to and through a life of joy, love, self-control. We are all responsible for how to live, love, and treat others. No one gets a free pass. Everyone's experience is different, yet the love of God is for all and the expectation for us is to do our best. Yes, change will make you vulnerable but fear from vulnerability can be overcome: "For God has not given us a spirit of timidity, but of power and love and discipline" (2 Tim 1:7).

High emotional intelligence is a product of "walking in the spirit". It encompasses self-esteem, self-control, peace, patience, goodness and kindness. High emotional intelligence is a way to freedom, Paul explains. If God's desire is for you to have characteristics that lead to successful living, why not go for it? The world would be a better place if we endeavor to be our best selves during our time in it. If we confess to being followers of God, then let us adopt Godly characteristics.

Increasing EI is not just for people who want to advance professionally. Those of us who care about spiritual growth and service should increase our EI too. We all need to become better at knowing how and when to extend grace, love more unselfishly, manage our emotions, and be better stewards of our spiritual gifts. Walking in the Spirit is a lifetime endeavor and "for all have sinned and fall short of the glory of God" (Rom 3:23). That means none of us are perfect, yet we are deserving of God's love and grace. Every person will have foibles and experience life's difficulties, yet as we purposely mature let them become less of a distraction to our daily lives, our successes and our relationships with other people.

Be a purveyor of hope. Paul ends a letter to the Christians at Rome with, "Now may the God of hope fill you with all joy and peace in believing, that you may abound in hope by the power of the Holy Spirit" (Rom 15:13). Boyatzis and McKee wrote, "Hope engages and raises our spirit and mobilizes energy. It causes us to want to act and enables us to draw on personal resources in the service of moving toward our goal."[1] Live in hope for your own future. Jeremiah wrote in 29:11 that God has a plan with benefits for you: "For I know the plans that I have for you,' declares the LORD, 'plans for welfare and not for calamity to give you a future and a hope" (Jer 29:11). Boyatzis and McKee go on to say, "A leader's hopeful outlook enables people to see beyond today's challenges to tomorrow's answers."[2]

As we master these virtues let us offer up our personal testimonies so that others may be encouraged. May your strengths always far outweigh your weaknesses, and God bless your efforts.

To God be the glory.

---

1. Boyatzis and McKee, *Resonant Leadership*, 75.
2. Boyatzis and McKee, *Resonant Leadership*, 75.

Bibliography

Boyatzis, Richard and Annie McKee. *Resonant Leadership*. Boston: Harvard Business School, 2005.

Bradberry, Travis, and Jean Greaves. *Emotional Intelligence 2.0*. San Diego: TalentSmart, 2009.

Braxton, Brad R. "Galatians." In *True to Our Native Land: An African American New Testament Commentary*, edited by Brian K. Blount, 333–47. Minneapolis: Fortress, 2007.

"Community." Oxford Dictionary https://www.oxfordlearnersdictionaries.com/us/definition/english/community?q=community.

Crowther, Steven S. "The Fruit of the Spirit in the Context of Leadership." *Journal of Biblical Perspectives in Leadership* 7.1 (Fall 2017) 24–34.

"Endorphins." Cleveland Clinic. https://my.clevelandclinic.org/health/body/23040-endorphins.

Foster, Richard. *Celebration of Discipline: The Path to Spiritual Growth*. New York: Harper Collins, 1998.

———. *Prayer: Finding the Heart's New Home*. New York: Harper Collins, 1982.

Frady, Kathy. "Spiritual Formation Parallels to Social-Emotional Learning Curriculum: A Contextual Analysis of 'Frog Street Curriculum.'" *International Journal of Children's Spirituality* 24.4 (2019) 401–14.

Francis (pope). *The Joy of the Gospel*. Frederick, MD: The Word Among Us, 2013.

Goleman, Daniel. *Emotional Intelligence: Why It Can Matter More Than IQ*. 10th anniversary edition. Random House: New York, 2005.

Goleman, Daniel, Richard Boyatzis, and Annie McGee. *Primal Leadership: Unleashing the Power of Emotional Intelligence*. 10th anniversary edition. Boston: Harvard Business Review, 2013.

Gunkel, Majaana, Christopher Schlaegel, and Vas Taras. "Cultural Values, Emotional Intelligence, and Conflict Handling Styles: A Global Study." *Journal of World Business* 51 (2016) 568–85.

Hosseinia, Shera, Samantha B. Meyer, and Mark Oremusba. "Is Your Religious Involvement Helping Your Mind? The Link Between Religious Involvement and Cognitive Function from the Perspective of Christian Pastors and Parishioners." *Journal of Religion, Spirituality & Aging* 34.3 (2022) 208–25.

Kelsey, James. "Practicing Civility in an Uncivil Age." *Review & Expositor* 116.2 2019, 146–59.

Kenneson, Phillip D. *Life on the Vine: Cultivating the Fruit of the Spirit.* InterVarsity: Downers Grove, 1999.

Kimmons, Matthew, and Douglas White. "Clergy Education and the Development of Emotional Intelligence: An Analysis of United Methodist Clergy In Kentucky." *Christian Education Journal: Research on Education Ministry* 16.2 (2019) 369–78.

Kirby, Jon P. "Inter-competencies for Religious Communities: Models, Gauges and Guides." *SEDOS Bulletin* 48.5 (May 6, 2016) 23–37.

Megreya, Ahmed. "Emotional Intelligence and Criminal Behavior." *Journal of Forensic Sciences* 60.1 (2015). https://onlinelibrary.wiley.com/doi/10.1111/1556-4029.12625.

Montaudon-Tomas, Cynthia M. "Avoiding Spiritual Bankruptcy in Organizations through the Fruit of the Spirit." *Journal of Biblical Perspectives in Leadership* 9.1 (Fall 2019) 17–34.

Mullainathan, Sendhil, and Eldar Shafir. *Scarcity: The New Science of Having Less and How It Defines Our Lives.* New York: Picador, 2013.

Noland, Rory. *The Heart of the Artist.* Grand Rapids: Zondervan, 2021.

Oliver, Morgan Richard. Twitter post. May 18, 2022, 10:42am, https://twitter.com/TheModernMorgan/status/1526936185901285376?lang=en

Oswald, Roy. "Emotional Intelligence and Congregational Leadership." *Reflective Practice* 36 (2016) 102–15.

Ott, Steven. "Emotional Intelligence and Leadership." *Congregations* 29.1 (Winter 2003) 20–21.

Painter, John. "The Fruit of the Spirit is Love: Galatians 5:22–23, An Exegetical Note." *Journal of Theology for Southern Africa* 5 (Dec 1973) 57–59.

Salomon, Sheryl Huggins. "Does Vitamin D Deficiency Pose a Special Risk for Black People?" Everyday Health. https://www.everydayhealth.com/vitamin-d/does-vitamin-d-deficiency-pose-a-special-risk-for-black-people/.

Samuels, Robyn. "Why Don't I Have an Appetite After Cooking?" Crush, Mar 7, 2023. https://crushmag-online.com/why-dont-i-have-an-appetite-after-cooking/.

Strauss, Barry. *Ten Caesars: Roman Emperors from Augustus to Constantine.* New York: Simon & Schuster, 2019.

TalentSmart. https://www.talentsmarteq.com/.

VIA Institute on Character. https://www.viacharacter.org/.

Wicks, Robert, and Tina Bucks. "Reframing for Change: The Use of Cognitive Behavioral Therapy and Native Psychology in Pastoral Ministry and Formation." *Human Development* 32 (Fall 2011) 9–14.

Wright, WJH. *Cultivating the Fruit of the Spirit: Growing in Christ Likeness.* Downers Grove: InterVarsity, 2017.

Young, Josiah U. III. "Self-Consciousness and Self-Control: Martin Luther King, Jr., A Drum Major for Nonviolence." *American Baptist Quarterly* 37.1 (Spring 2018) 70–82.

"Yes, Weather Can Affect Mood and Energy—And So Can Climate Change." Healthline, Aug 12, 2022. https://www.healthline.com/health/mental-health/weather-and-mood#the-effects.